The Path ...... *the Peacemakers*

The Triumph over Terrorism of the Church in Peru

DAVID MILLER

David Miller, an American, has lived in Bolivia since 1981, working as a missionary with the Church of God. An itinerant evangelist and Bible teacher among the indigenous Andean peoples, he also freelances for various Christian news agencies. David and his wife, Barbara, are the parents of four children.

TRIANGLE

First published in Great Britain in 2001 by
Triangle
SPCK
Holy Trinity Church
Marylebone Road
London NW1 4DU

British Library Cataloguing-in-Publication Data

A catalogue record for this book is available
from the British Library

ISBN 0–281–05318–9

Typeset by Pioneer Associates, Perthshire
Printed in Great Britain by
Omnia Books, Glasgow

Contents

Acknowledgements

The author would like to thank the many people who granted personal interviews in the preparation of this book, and acknowledge the following written sources, which provided valuable information on Peru and Shining Path.

Degregori, Carlos Ivan (1990) *Ayacucho 1969–1979: El Surgimiento de Sendero Luminoso*, Lima: Instituto de Estudios Peruanos.

Degregori, Carlos Ivan, with Jose Coronel, Ponciano del Pino, Orin Starn (1996) *Las Rondas Campesinas y la Derrota de Sendero Luminoso*, Lima: Instituto de Estudios Peruanos.

López, Darío (1998) *Los Evangélicos y los Derechos Humanos; La experiencia social del Concilio Nacional Evangélico del Perú 1980–1992*, Lima: Centro Evangélico de Misiología Andina-Amazónica (CEMAA).

For readers who would like to do more research into the evangelical church and the Shining Path war, the author recommends these fine books:

Maust, John (1987) *Peace and Hope in the Corner of the Dead*, Miami, FL: Latin America Mission.

Whalin, W. Terry and Woehr, Chris (1993) *One Bright Shining Path*, Wheaton, IL: Crossway Books.

To Sarah, Benjamin,
Molly and Carmen,
four of the best

Behold, I cry out, 'Violence!' but I am not answered;
I call aloud, but there is no justice.
He has walled up my way, so that I cannot pass,
and he has set darkness upon my paths.

(Job 19.7–8)

Oh that my words were written!
Oh that they were inscribed in a book!
Oh that with an iron pen and lead they were graven
in the rock for ever!
For I know that my Redeemer lives,
and at last he will stand upon the earth.

(Job 19.23–26)

List of Characters

Alfonso, Torribio. Pastor of the Ashaninka Evangelical Church in Poyeni.

Arana, Pedro. Vice-president of the National Council of Evangelicals of Peru (CONEP) and founding chairman of the Peace and Hope Commission.

Araujo, Badd. Itinerant evangelist in Tingo Maria who shared Christ with guerrilla commander Jorge Rios.

Artaza, Alvaro (Captain). Commander of the Marine Infantry patrol who murdered six members of the Presbyterian Church in Callqui in 1984.

Aurelio, Alejandro. Christian leader from Potsoteni who organized covert evacuation of Christian families from the village in February 1989. Brother of Pedro Aurelio.

Aurelio, Pedro. Ashaninka evangelist from Potsoteni and theology student at the Swiss Indian Mission near Pucallpa. Brother of Alejandro Aurelio.

Belaúnde Terry, Fernando. President of Peru, 1980–1985.

Benson, Bruce. American missionary abducted by Shining Path in Llata, May 1981.

Benson, Jan (Mrs Bruce). American missionary abducted by Shining Path in Llata, May 1981.

Calderón, Alejandro. Great Chief of the Ashaninka. Abducted and later murdered by guerrillas of the Tupac Amaru Revolutionary Movement (MRTA) in 1989.

Cecilio, Natividad Aranibar (Mrs). Wife of Pablo Cecilio, pastor of the Ashaninka Evangelical Church. Taken prisoner by Shining Path in 1991.

Cecilio, Pablo. Pastor of the Ashaninka Evangelical Church. Taken prisoner by Shining Path in 1991.

Chuchón, Avilio. Son of Juan Carlos and Pelagia Chuchón.

Chuchón, Juan Carlos. Bricklayer, originally from San Francisco de Pujas, Ayacucho. Arrested with his wife, Pelagia, in December 1992 and imprisoned in Yanomayo for treason against the state.

Chuchón, Marlene. Daughter of Juan Carlos and Pelagia Chuchón.

Chuchón, Pelagia Salcedo (Mrs). Mother of three. Arrested with her husband, Juan Carlos, in December 1992 and imprisoned in Chorrillos for treason against the state.

Coveña, Cornejo (Colonel). Governor of Chorrillos prison.

Curi, Teófila. Evangelical believer imprisoned in Chorrillos with Mrs Antonia Jaimes.

Diaz, Augosto. Pastor of the Ashaninka Evangelical Church in Tsiriari. Driven into exile with his family when Shining Path occupied the village in May 1990.

Efraín (surname withheld). Jorge Rios's bodyguard in San Jorge.

Emerson, Homer. American missionary and linguist. Collaborated with Rómulo and Donna Sauñe on the translation of the Ayacucho Bible.

Fajardo, Alfredo. Accompanied Rómulo Sauñe on final visit to Chakiqpampa in September 1992. Later joined staff of *Runa Simi*.

Fajardo, Margarita (Mrs Alfredo). Accompanied Rómulo Sauñe on final visit to Chakiqpampa in September 1992.

Ferreira, Pedro. Director of Pacific Radio in Lima. Launched national prayer movement in May 1989 to intercede for the pacification of Peru.

Friesen, Maurine (Mrs Paul). American missionary and mother of five. Began working among the Ashaninka in 1960.

Friesen, Paul. American missionary and Bible professor. Began working among the Ashaninka in 1960.

Fujimori, Alberto. President of Peru, elected 1990.

Guzman Reynoso, Abimael. Former philosophy professor at the National University of San Cristobal of Huamanga in Ayacucho. Founded Shining Path in 1970.

Izarra, Simon. Quechua preacher in Ayacucho who prayed with Justiniano Quicaña to receive Christ.

Jaimes, Antonia Alfaro (Mrs). Arrested with her husband, Benito, in November 1992 and imprisoned in Chorrillos on terrorist charges.

Jaimes, Benito. Arrested with his wife, Antonia, in November 1992 and imprisoned in Castro Castro on terrorist charges.

Jaimes, Kelly. Eldest daughter of Benito and Antonia Jaimes.

Jaimes, Rodolfo. Eldest son of Benito and Antonia Jaimes.

Mallea, Cristina (Mrs Juan). Lima schoolteacher who asked the Peace and Hope Commission to defend her husband against terrorist charges.

Mallea, Juan. Lima taxi-driver arrested in July 1993 and accused of participating in the Cantuta University massacre.

Matías, Ruben. Blind pastor of the Christian and Missionary Alliance Church. Led Jorge Rios to Christ in San Jorge.

Meza, Caleb. Successor to Pedro Arana as chairman of the Peace and Hope Commission.

Mora, José Pablo. Veteran human-rights attorney retained by the Peace and Hope Commission to defend Juan Mallea.

Palomino, Miguel Angel. President of CONEP who helped organize the Peace and Hope Commission.

Paredes, Tito. Co-founder, with Pedro Arana, of the Peace and Hope Commission.

Pérez, Rolando. Lima journalist and staff member of the Peace and Hope Commission.

Phelps, Conrad. American missionary and linguist. Collaborated with Rómulo and Donna Sauñe on the translation of the Ayacucho Bible.

Phelps, Irma (Mrs Conrad). Native of Cuzco. Collaborated with Rómulo and Donna Sauñe on the translation of the Ayacucho Bible.

Pinazo, Marco Antonio Quicaña. Grandson of Justiniano and Teofila Quicaña. Murdered by Shining Path, along with three other male relatives, on 5 September 1992.

Presidente Gonzalo. Code name for Shining Path founder, Abimael Guzman.

Quicaña, (Miguel) Arcangel. Second eldest son of Justiniano and Teofila Quicaña. Survived Shining Path ambush on 5 September 1992, in which four male relatives died. Later elected to the Peruvian congress.

Quicaña Jaulis, Antonia (Mrs). Third eldest daughter of Justiniano and Teofila Quicaña. Shining Path murdered her son, Josué, and three other male relatives on 5 September 1992.

Quicaña, Fernando. Eldest son of Justiniano and Teofila Quicaña. With his mother, accepted Christ in 1957 in Chakiqpampa.

Quicaña, Justiniano. Quechua farmer/shepherd and Christian evangelist from Chakiqpampa, Ayacucho. Descendant of Huaman Inca Quicaña.

Quicaña, Teofila Aviles (Mrs Justiniano). First evangelical Christian convert in Chakiqpampa. Mother of Zoila, Fernando, Rufina, Antonia and Miguel Arcangel Quicaña.

Regalado, José. Lima attorney and staff member of Peace and Hope Commission.

Regalado, Ruth Alvarado (Mrs José). Lima attorney and staff member of Peace and Hope Commission.

Rios, Isabel del Carmen Santamaría (Mrs). Married Jorge Rios in December 1993, Buenos Aires.

Rios, Jorge. Shining Path guerrilla who participated in the kidnapping of Bruce, Jan and Bryan Benson. Later commanded a rebel battalion in San Jorge.

Saico, Vicente. Director of a Christian radio station in Huanta. First to expose publicly the murders of six members of the Presbyterian Church in nearby Callqui.

Santoma, Rafael. Ashaninka evangelist from Camajeni whose brother, Pablo, was killed by Shining Path.

Sauñe, Demetrio. First cousin of Rómulo, Joshua and Ruben Sauñe. Confronted Shining Path over land dispute in Ayacucho.

Sauñe, Donna Jackson (Mrs). Daughter of American missionaries. Married Rómulo Sauñe in 1977 and now directs *Runa Simi*.

Sauñe, Enrique. Quechua Christian evangelist from Chakiqpampa, Ayacucho. Father of Rómulo, Joshua and Ruben Sauñe.

Sauñe, Joshua. Grandson of Justiniano Quicaña. Younger brother of Rómulo Sauñe and now on staff of *Runa Simi*.

Sauñe, Lorenzo and Guadalupe. Quechua Christians from Chakiqpampa, Ayacucho. Parents of Enrique Sauñe.

Sauñe, Missy Aspa (Mrs). Native of Arizona, USA. Married Joshua Sauñe in 1988.

Sauñe, Rómulo. Grandson of Justiniano Quicaña. Quechua Bible translator and founder, with wife Donna, of *Runa Simi*.

Sauñe, Ruben. Grandson of Justiniano Quicaña. Younger brother of Rómulo and Joshua Sauñe.

Sauñe, Zoila Quicaña (Mrs Enrique). Eldest daughter of Justiniano and Teofila Quicaña. Mother of Rómulo, Joshua and Ruben Sauñe.

Trisollini, Carlos. Quechua-Italian native of Ayacucho. Boyhood friend of Joshua and Ruben Sauñe.

Vargas, Germán. Lima attorney and staff member of Peace and Hope Commission.

Velando, Máximo. Guerrilla leader of the Movement of the Revolutionary Left. Staged a short-lived uprising in 1965.

Wieland, Alfonso. Successor to Caleb Meza as director of the Peace and Hope Commission.

Yupanqui, Lea. Granddaughter of Justiniano and Teofila Quicaña. Abducted and tortured by the military in November 1982 while a student at the National University of San Cristobal of Huamanga in Ayacucho.

Yupanqui, Rafael. Presbyterian pastor (itinerant) in district of Ayacucho. Father of Lea Yupanqui.

Yupanqui, Rufina Quicaña (Mrs Rafael). Second eldest daughter of Justiniano and Teofila Quicaña and mother of Lea Yupanqui.

Map of Peru

1

A Day with Terrorists

Huamalies, 31 May 1989

Bruce Benson could not believe it was happening.

The time was around 8.00 a.m. He, Jan and their 14-year-old son Bryan had been on the road for two hours, heading back to Huánuco. The Bensons, missionaries with Wycliffe Bible Translators, had spent the past fortnight in Llata, a small town high in the Peruvian Andes. During their stay, they had participated in conferences of the Christian and Missionary Alliance Church and worked on a Quechua translation of the Scriptures. They were anxious to get home and see their daughters, Kristen and Kara, who had stayed in Huánuco with family friends.

But the Bensons would not make it home that day.

Rounding a curve, Bruce had to brake suddenly to avoid colliding with a flatbed truck that straddled the narrow dirt road. Within seconds, young men and women in army fatigues began cascading off the sides of the truck. They surrounded the Bensons' car and pointed their automatic weapons in the faces of the three people inside.

'Get out! Get out!' they shouted. 'We're going to burn your car!'

Bruce realized immediately they were Shining Path guerrillas. He mouthed a brief prayer, perhaps his last. Everything he knew about the Path told him they would next drag him, Jan and Bryan to the side of the road and kill them.

The faces of Kristen and Kara receiving the news of their parents' death flashed through Jan Benson's mind. Even more frightening to her in that instant was the thought of watching Bryan die at the hands of the terrorists. Or perhaps the boy would be forced to witness his parents being tortured or perhaps dismembered. She too prayed a brief, desperate prayer: 'Lord, help us please.'

As the terrorists closed in, Jan heard Bryan say softly: 'I love you, Jesus.'

'Who are you and what are you doing here?' a terrorist demanded of Bruce when he stepped out of the car.

'We're missionaries,' Bruce replied. 'We are on our way home from Llata.'

He looked around at his captors. There were about 45 guerrillas, some of them not much older than Bryan. All of them toted automatic weapons, sidearms and knives. Some carried grenades, dynamite and plastic explosives. They obviously had come to do battle with forces greater than a family of three.

*   *   *

Shining Path, in fact, existed to do battle with the nation of Peru. Abimael Guzman Reynoso, a philosophy professor from Ayacucho and disenchanted member of the Communist Party, launched the movement in 1970, soon after being jailed in Lurigancho Prison for helping organize anti-government protests among peasant farmers. As a loyal communist, Guzman based his vision of a socialist utopia upon the teachings of Karl Marx. As a radical communist, he borrowed his revolutionary methods from the teachings of Mao Zedong.

Mao's teachings, of course, had inspired the Cultural Revolution in China. That attempt to reinvent Chinese society was in full swing when Guzman began to draw up the blueprints for the Shining Path insurrection. He visited the People's Republic twice during his formative years to study Mao's thought and learn terrorist tactics. Through his studies and first-hand experience, the philosopher from Ayacucho became enamoured of Mao's radical doctrine of 'zero-based revolution'.

Zero-based revolution was the defining quality that set Shining Path apart from every other terrorist movement, past and present, that Latin America has endured. Other guerrilla groups appeared moderate or even humane compared to

Shining Path. The Tupac Aymaru Revolutionary Movement, or MRTA as it was known by its Spanish acronym, operated in Peru contemporaneously with Shining Path and sometimes cooperated with Guzman's followers. But the alliance could never be lasting, since the goal of MRTA was only to bring the state to its knees and force the government to negotiate its demands for changes in Peru's social structure. Shining Path, on the other hand, would stop only when it had totally annihilated the government, the state and Peru's existing social structure.

Just as the Cultural Revolution had attempted to turn the social clock back to zero in China by destroying society, then rebuild it into a socialist utopia, so Shining Path set out to reduce Peru to a pre-civilized state in order to recreate the country in the image of Communism. This was the ideal. The reality was quite different. The sorrow, suffering and hardship visited upon the People's Republic of China during the years of the Cultural Revolution are impossible to calculate. In Peru's case, government bureaucrats crunched the numbers and estimated, more or less, how much the Shining Path revolution cost: 25,000 dead, 50,000 orphans, 1 million refugees, 25 billion dollars.

Shining Path engineered this appalling national disaster with the support of a tiny minority of the country's population. In the two decades that he headed the movement, Guzman succeeded in recruiting only between 10,000 and 15,000 guerrillas into Shining Path. The vast majority were university students, peasant farmers and teenagers. He forged them into a ruthless fighting force through ceaseless indoctrination, strict discipline and brutal punishment for insubordination. The rank and file of Shining Path terrorists never met Guzman personally, nor even saw a photograph of the man. They referred to him always by a code name: 'Presidente Gonzalo'. Despite the lack of personal contact – or perhaps because of it – they developed fierce loyalty to their revolutionary leader.

Partido Comunista de Peru Sendero Luminoso was the full Spanish name Guzman gave to his organization. In casual conversation, Peruvians shortened it simply to *Sendero*, 'the Path'.

Following customary Spanish usage, the movement's followers then became known as *senderistas*.

*   *   *

Few people who fell into the hands of the *senderistas* on deserted roads in the middle of the Andes lived to tell it, especially if they were unarmed foreigners. The weekend before the Path captured the Bensons, British citizen Edward Collins Barthley, 25, of Chester was on a backpacking tour of the Huaraz highlands. He stopped in the small town of Olleros to spend the night in one of the municipal buildings. The Path invaded and surprised Barthley, whom they shot in the leg when he tried to bolt from the building. The terrorists then dragged the young backpacker to the town square and shot him through the heart.

The same week in the mountains near Ayacucho, the Path captured Barbara D'Achille, Peru's leading environmental journalist, who was writing a feature news report on an agricultural project in the area. The *senderistas* demanded D'Achille write a feature article on them, one that would present the Path to the world in a heroic light. She flatly refused, adding her personal opinion of the Path and Presidente Gonzalo. Her opinion did not please the *senderistas*, who responded by brutally torturing Ms D'Achille and then stoning her to death.

This morning, Bruce, Jan and Bryan Benson stood together on the road while the *senderistas* discussed what to do with the family.

'Take your things out of the vehicle,' they ordered. 'We are going to burn it.'

The Bensons started to unload their cargo, an electric generator, movie projector, films, suitcases and boxes of household goods they were moving from a cottage near Llata, where they customarily stayed on trips into the mountains, back to their home in Huánuco. They had removed a few of the items when the *senderistas* changed their minds.

'Leave the things there,' they said. 'We are going to take your car. Get in the truck, you're coming with us.'

Jan Benson climbed into the back of the truck and sat down

on one of the bench seats arranged there. This was one of the most frightening moments she had ever faced. She wondered if the Path would choose a more opportune moment to kill them, perhaps in public, before a crowd of rural peasants, having first condemned them as hated Yankee imperialists. Or perhaps this was the beginning of months of captivity. She assumed they would kill Bruce, Bryan and her, but would they torture them first? She again began to pray, silently.

'You there, get in beside me,' one of the guerrillas said to Bruce. 'We're going to talk.' Bruce climbed into the front seat between the driver and the guerrilla commander. The small caravan headed down the narrow dirt road back to Llata.

'Who are you and what are you doing here?' the guerrilla asked Bruce.

'As I said before, we are missionaries. We have been working these past weeks in Llata. We were on our way home just now.'

'Religious people, eh?' the guerrilla said. 'We believe, with Marx, that religion is the opiate of the people. However, we're willing to allow people to choose. If they choose that, well, it's their business. But we don't believe it does them any good.'

Bruce felt his tense muscles relax a bit. It appeared the young man did not hate him all that much. He ventured a reply.

'In the time I've been out here working with these people, I've found that life is tough. But the people who have religion in their lives have hope. It gives them something to live for.'

'Nah, I don't believe that,' his seat mate said. 'Religion is of little use to anybody.'

Over the next two hours, Bruce carried on an intermittent discussion of religion and politics with the young man. The conversation did little to convince either of them to change their views on these matters, but Bruce felt that the more he communicated on a personal level with his captors, the better were the family's chances of survival.

Meanwhile, Jan engaged one of the young women in conversation in the back of the truck. She learned that the Path was on its way to 'liberate' Llata, the provincial capital of Huamalies. That explained why the *senderistas* were so heavily armed. However, they encountered no soldiers or police on the journey, so the liberation would be a peaceful one. This was the first answer to Jan's prayers.

The townspeople of Llata were shocked to see the Benson family, who had left only a few hours before, pull into town that morning with the Path. Small squadrons of guerrilla fighters dropped off at different public offices to secure the buildings and cut communication with the outside world. Some seized the hospital, emptying the dispensary of medicine. Others went door to door ordering Llata residents to close up their shops and homes and gather in the plaza for a general meeting.

As the flatbed truck passed the municipal building, Jan recognized the mayor, tied up, standing in the doorway. A girl sitting near her remarked that the Path was planning to kill the mayor, following a revolutionary trial, of course. Once more, Jan began to pray silently.

Huamanga, 1989

The peasant farmers and shepherds of Paccha were still sleeping in the early hours of that December morning when some one hundred Shining Path guerrillas stole into town. The *senderistas* went house to house, rousing families from their beds and herding them at gunpoint into the village plaza. There, the people of Paccha listened in numb silence to a speech by the guerrilla commander.

He said the Path had come to Paccha in the interests of 'revolutionary justice'. The villagers' offence, he said, was co-operating with the Armed Forces of Peru to organize a militia – a Civil Defence Committee as it was officially known – to protect their town. This amounted to rebellion against the Path and would not be tolerated. The farmers and shepherds did not deny the charges. Of course they had formed a civilian militia. The army would have punished them as guerrilla sympathizers had they not done so.

The gruff commander then read a list of names compiled by Shining Path infiltrators who had been spying on Paccha and surrounding communities in recent months. Guerrillas pulled the men, 22 town leaders and youthful militia members, from the crowd. They tied their hands behind them and threw them face down to the ground. While this was happening, other *senderistas* conducted the women and children to rooms in a nearby building. There they could not see, but did hear, what happened next.

The women and children heard no shooting. 'We do not waste bullets on the likes of you,' the *senderistas* told the men lying prostrate in the plaza. 'We save our ammunition for more important targets.'

This claim was partly true. The Path had learned that more economical methods of murder were the most terrifying. Terrorists formed their reputation for cruelty with atrocities like the one committed on a narrow highway running up from the jungle to the highlands. One night near Tapuna, a truck driver came across eight young men lying face down on the roadway. He braked in time to avoid running over them. Suddenly, he was looking down the barrels of several *senderista* guns. They ordered him to keep driving. He protested, his stomach churning at the thought of what that would mean. The terrorists gave him a choice. Either he could drive over the men lying on the roadway, or the *senderistas* would shoot him and do the driving themselves. The truck driver gulped, closed his eyes and threw his rig into gear. He did not stop until he had put several miles between himself and Tapuna. Later he learned that the terrorists had obliged a second truck driver to run over the eight victims to finish them off, but the report did not console the poor man.

The women and children in Paccha did hear screaming that December morning. It lasted for half an hour, while *senderistas* smashed heavy rocks on the skulls of the 22 men and youths lying in the plaza. Some of the peasant farmers did not die easily, forcing the terrorists to use bayonets and machetes to finish the task.

The Path slipped out of the village with the rising sun. The *senderistas* left as quietly as they had come, heading north on foot towards their base in Huancavelica, hoping to arrive there before the army dispatched helicopter gunships to pursue them. Behind the silent marchers rose the doleful cries of newly widowed wives and orphaned sons and daughters.

While this tragedy unfolded in Paccha, *senderistas* were visiting similar revolutionary justice on the nearby villages of Andabamba and Ccahuiñayocc. Because these communities were smaller, and because some of the peasant farmers and shepherds there had relatives among the guerrillas, Andabamba and Ccahuiñayocc lost only 11 men each.

Further away lay the village of Chakiqpampa, which had learned that the Path was coming before the guerrillas slipped into town that morning. By then, all the men of Chakiqpampa had fled into the mountains, except for 85-year-old Justiniano Quicaña. A peace-loving Christian evangelist, Justiniano assumed that the Path would not bother killing one so elderly as he. In this, he was mistaken.

*   *   *

When the Bensons reached the plaza of Llata, their Christian friends began to gather around them, asking if they needed help.

'Please, keep your distance,' the Bensons advised. 'It's best if the *senderistas* do not identify you as friends of ours.' Although they expected to die, Bruce and Jan did not want to take any of the Christians of Llata with them.

When all one thousand citizens of Llata had gathered in the square, the meeting commenced. A guerrilla commander stood up on a table and announced who the intruders were: a popular Marxist-Leninist-Maoist revolutionary army, dedicated to 'the thought of Presidente Gonzalo'. The speaker then led the people in a mandatory salute to Abimael Guzman. Everyone raised his right fist in the air and shouted, 'Long live the President! Long live Gonzalo!' The townspeople listened quietly to the guerrilla's rendition of a hymn to international revolution. The Path lowered the Peruvian flag that flew in the middle of the plaza and ran up a little red flag displaying the hammer and sickle.

After several hours of speeches, the terrorists announced a 'revolutionary trial' of Llata civic officials. The mayor, still tied,

was led before the crowd. Jan Benson prayed even more fer-
vently now. This was the dreaded moment she knew blood
would be shed, a moment her 14-year-old son would be forced
to witness.

Ayacucho, 1986

Demetrio Sauñe knows that prayer can help one's chances
when facing revolutionary justice. Demetrio was 28 years old
and married with two small children when he received a letter
from the Path telling him he had three days to disappear from
Ayacucho or he would be killed.

'What in the world have you done?' sobbed his wife Victoria,
when he told her of the notice.

'It's the problem with the abandoned lots in the Licenciado
Borough,' he explained. 'One of the absentee owners complained to the *senderistas* about me.'

As chairman of the Veterans Association Housing Commission, Demetrio had been dealing with the problem in the
Licenciado Borough for nearly a year. The government had
carved the new neighbourhood out of empty land on the city's
edge to benefit former soldiers and their families. For payment
of a monthly quota, which mainly went to finance water and
electric utilities, each family received title to 1,700 square feet
of land on which to build a home. Most veterans that received
land paid their dues regularly. The problem arose with absentee owners, many of whom had moved away from Ayacucho
because of Shining Path violence. They stopped paying their
quotas, obliging the rest of the veterans to pay higher dues. In
one of their monthly assemblies, the veterans directed the
chairman of the housing commission to resolve the problem.

Demetrio did what was customary and legal. A notice
appeared in the Ayacucho papers notifying lot owners that
they had six months to pay delinquent quotas, or else they
would lose title to their properties. When the six months
expired, the newspaper announced a grace period of three
months more. When the grace period had expired, Demetrio
announced a three-week extension. Only when that had

lapsed did the Veterans Association finally move to confiscate the abandoned lots of some 32 owners who had made no effort to pay their fees.

But one of the veterans who lost his land complained to a relative in the Path that he had been unfairly treated by Demetrio Sauñe. He also alleged, falsely, that Demetrio was selling the lots and pocketing the proceeds. Stealing, along with murder and lying, was one of the three cardinal sins that the Path punished with death.

There were other sins, as well. Demetrio knew one man whom the Path killed for threatening to beat his wife. In another incident, a youth charged with molesting a neighbour girl was executed in front of the offended family, who later admitted he was probably innocent after all. Hundreds of Ayacucho residents had suffered brutal retribution for offences much less serious than that for which Demetrio stood accused.

'Three days is not enough time to sell our house and move away,'Victoria told her husband.'What are you going to do?'

'I'm going to meet with the *senderistas*,' Demetrio said. 'I want to explain the facts to them.'

'You're crazy!'Victoria's eyes widened in disbelief.'They will kill you for sure!' She started weeping again.

Demetrio placed a hand on his wife's shoulder.'It will be all right. I have a clear conscience in regard to this matter. I have done nothing wrong.'

'You must understand something, my love,' he added. 'If I disappear from Ayacucho, they will interpret it as an admission of guilt. We will be running from the Path for the rest of our lives. And sooner or later, they will catch up to us. This is really the only solution.'

Demetrio contacted the Path through an intermediary in his neighbourhood and arranged to meet with them in Yura Yura at 3.00 p.m. on the third and final day. When he left home, Victoria started weeping.'Don't worry, my love, nothing is going to happen to me,' he said.

'The children and I will be here praying,'Victoria said, still weeping.

Demetrio found the address in Yura Yura and was ushered through a long, gloomy corridor to a room in the back of the building. Eight solemn young men were waiting for him there. They asked Demetrio to explain his side of the housing commission problem.

He took his time, careful to document his version of events with dates, minutes of association meetings and copies of court papers. When he mentioned the sale of the abandoned lots, one of the young men asked him: 'What have you done with the money?'

'The association used it to buy water and electric meters for the borough, as well as for other improvements. Here, I brought the receipts with me.'

The *senderistas* looked at the receipts, then looked at one another. It seemed to them that Demetrio was, in fact, telling the truth. 'Tell us more about your work with the housing commission,' they said.

Demetrio answered their questions as thoroughly as possible. The longer he talked, the more he relaxed. 'Maybe I will survive this meeting after all,' he thought to himself. He looked at his watch. It was 9.00 p.m.

'Comrade, we are convinced that you have done nothing wrong,' his interrogators finally told him. 'You may keep on working. You have nothing to fear from us and you are free to go now.'

A relieved Demetrio stood up and began to shake hands around the room.

'Ah, one more thing,' his interrogators said. Demetrio stopped shaking hands. 'Never forget, the Path has a thousand eyes and a thousand ears. See to it that you make no mistakes.'

When Demetrio walked through the door of his home, he found Victoria and the children still on their knees, praying. Victoria screamed when she saw her husband – from surprise as much as from sheer joy.

She hugged Demetrio tight. 'We didn't think we would ever see you again. All evening I've been trying to figure out how to make a life for myself as a widow with two small children.'

'I told you we had nothing to worry about,' Demetrio said. 'After all, the Lord is with us, isn't he?'

Then it was his turn to weep.

*   *   *

Jan Benson is convinced that what happened in Llata was nothing short of a miracle. The Path brought the mayor before the revolutionary tribunal that afternoon and read the charges against him. They were the standard charges: official corruption, neglect of duties, acting against the best interests of the people. Then, as was the custom in people's trials, they asked if anyone in the crowd had anything to say.

Several Llata residents, in fact, did have things to say about their mayor. He was a good mayor, they said, and a good man. Maybe in other towns they had corruption and neglect, but in Llata they had no such thing. The terrorists listened to the testimonies. Did they consider the mayor an enemy of the revolution? they asked Llata residents. Of course not, they replied. He wants only our welfare, just as you do. In the face of such compelling evidence, the Path had no alternative but to declare the mayor innocent. They cut his bonds and set him free.

In that moment, Jan Benson knew God himself was present in Llata. There was no other explanation.

Later that afternoon, the Bensons saw their car stop at the edge of the plaza. All day the *senderistas* had been using it to ferry people back and forth to the town meeting. This time when the car stopped, a guerrilla in the front seat gestured to Bruce. Bruce walked over to the car and faced a man he had never seen before, sitting in the front seat between the driver and a young girl. To Bruce, he seemed the personification of evil.

'Who are you really?' the man asked.

'I've already told your comrades who I am,' Bruce replied. 'I am a missionary and I work with the churches out here. We do scripture translation and literacy training. We've lived here for a long time.'

The man stared at Bruce for a few seconds. 'Then who are these Belgians?' he demanded. 'Are you Belgian?'

'No, I'm not Belgian.'

The *senderista* pondered this. 'We're going to take your car,' he said abruptly.

'Well, I don't understand that,' Bruce said. 'I just heard your own comrades explain the rules. They say that if you borrow something, you're supposed to give it back. I've loaned you my car all day long and now you tell me you're going to take it? That doesn't sound right to me.'

He had no idea why he was arguing with this man. Bruce knew the *senderista* commander would kill him in an instant, with no qualms whatsoever, if it pleased him to do so. But then the man's evil stare broke into an indulgent smile. He shook his head, as if dismissing a complaint from a foolish child.

'No, no, you don't understand,' he said. 'We're not borrowing your car; we're confiscating it in the name of the revolution. This car now belongs to the people. You're an imperialist. Why, you don't even belong in this country. So, we're taking your car.'

Bruce took exception to being labelled an imperialist.

'I am no imperialist,' he protested. 'I don't live in the city. I don't hang about with rich people. I work out here in the boondocks with the poor. I have, in fact, many of the same goals as you, to alleviate suffering and injustice. We just go about it in different ways.'

The man's indulgent smile faded. 'Yes, you are an imperialist. The very fact that you have enough money to come to a foreign country to work means that you are an imperialist.'

The man looked hard at Bruce. 'We're taking your car. It's enough that we're leaving you here alive.'

Bruce said nothing, but to himself was thinking, 'Sounds like a good trade to me.'

The man pointed to the boxes full of the Bensons' belongings. 'What is all this stuff?' he asked.

'Oh, it's just some junk we were taking back home.'

'We're going to go through it.' He directed Bruce to a nearby house where the guerrillas helped him unload the entire cargo. They found the Bensons' electric generator and movie projector.

'Does this stuff work?' the guerrilla commander asked.

'Yeah, but not too well. I've had nothing but trouble with it. You wouldn't want to take it.'

'Sure we would. We can use this to show revolutionary films.' The guerrillas started carrying the generator and the movie projector out to their truck.

Bruce felt frustration welling up inside him again. 'Well, if you're going to take the projector, you might as well take the films, too,' he said.

'You mean, you have films to go with this?'

'Yes, I have some wonderful films, colour films. You'll enjoy them.'

Bruce handed the man six reels, his entire series on the Gospel of Luke. 'You be sure and watch these,' he said, smiling.

At 6 o'clock that evening, the entire squadron of *senderistas* left Llata in the flatbed truck and the Bensons' car. Bruce, Jan and Bryan hugged one another, happy to be alive and together, despite being left with no car, no money and no way home.

The family's Christian friends gathered round them. 'Please, come spend the night with us,' one man urged. The Bensons gratefully accepted the offer. After the evening meal, the Bensons sat around the table with their fellow believers talking about the extraordinary events of the day. The shock and stress gradually wore off as they prayed together.

Though they were poor themselves, the Christians of Llata offered to do what they could to help the Bensons reach home safely. Returning to Huánuco was out of the question, since the terrorists would still be roaming the roads in that direction. The little group decided the missionary family should travel by bus to Lima. Those who could gave the Bensons money for the fare. It was not enough, so the next morning, their Christian friends went to the terminal and talked with the agent at the bus company. They assured him that the Bensons were trustworthy people and would pay the remainder of their fare upon arrival in Lima. The agent agreed to reserve seats for them on the next bus, two days hence.

Meanwhile, Gomer Cruz, an itinerant pastor to some 30 Christian and Missionary Alliance churches in the area surrounding Llata, carried a letter to Lima, informing mission headquarters of the ordeal. Lima then called Huánuco to tell Kristen and Kara what had happened and to assure them that their parents and brother were all right. The note also explained the Bensons' plan to travel to Lima and instructed the girls to join their parents there.

After an emotional family reunion at the Lima bus terminal, the Bensons took several days to rest in the capital before returning home to Huánuco. A few months later, the family moved from Huánuco to Lima. The mission had asked Bruce to assume administrative duties at field headquarters. A year later, through a remarkable series of events, the Bensons would learn exactly how close they had come to dying that day in Llata at the hands of Shining Path.

2

The Incas of Huamanga

Shining Path was born in Ayacucho, a city that lies on a direct south-east line between Lima, the capital of Peru, and Cuzco, the capital of the ancient Inca empire. The overland route to Ayacucho is nothing close to a direct line, however. The road from Lima follows the coastline south through the Atacama desert, turns inland at Pisco and winds up and over the ridge of the Andes, attaining heights near 16,000 feet above sea level before dropping sharply into the upper basin of the Apurimac River. Ayacucho, a city of 200,000 residents, occupies a broad valley in the upper reaches of the basin.

The Incas knew this area as 'Huamanga' or 'Place of the Hawk'. After the Spanish conquered Peru and made the region into a colonial department, or state, its official name became 'Ayacucho', which means 'Corner of the Dead'. The title is suggestive of a local inclination to violence. For centuries before the coming of the Spanish, rival Indian clans here carried on blood feuds. In the early years of the colony, Ayacucho witnessed civil wars between rival Spanish generals. Ayacucho even experienced revolution long before Shining Path appeared. In 1824, Simón Bolívar and Antonio José de Sucre won the decisive battle ending South America's War of Independence just outside the town.

The ancient Inca title for the area survives, however, most notably in the name of the National University of San Cristobal of Huamanga, the school where Abimael Guzman taught philosophy before he launched Shining Path. The principal province of the department of Ayacucho also carries the name 'Huamanga'. Huamanga Province stretches westward from the department capital over high ridges of the Andes and into the Cachi River valley. Native Americans inhabit, almost exclusively, the peasant farms and adobe villages of rural Huamanga. Instead of Spanish, the modern language of Peru, rural Huamangans speak Quechua, the language of the ancient Inca empire. This is why their countrymen refer to them, and they refer to themselves, as 'Quechuas'.

Justiniano Quicaña was born in the village of Chakiqpampa, Huamanga Province, in 1904. Justiniano was a direct descendant of an Inca general who settled there in the sixteenth century after fleeing the Spanish occupation of Cuzco. He knew well the history of his clan and relished passing on the story to his grandchildren.

'We Quicañas are children of Huaman Inca Quicaña, who was descended from the first Inca ruler, Manco Capaq. The Spanish would have killed Huaman Inca Quicaña, had they been able to catch him, just as they killed the last Inca ruler, Atahualpa. But Quicaña outsmarted the Spaniards by running away to Copacabana, a haven on Lake Titicaca. By the time the Europeans discovered Copacabana, Huaman Inca Quicaña had moved his people here to Huamanga.'

Three of Justiniano's grandsons, Rómulo, Joshua and Ruben Sauñe, relished hearing the stories of their Inca ancestors. Their mother, Zoila, eldest daughter of Justiniano and his wife Teofila, was married to Enrique Sauñe, eldest son of Lorenzo and Guadalupe Suañe. The Sauñes could also claim Inca ancestry. Many of their neighbours in Huamanga, however, could not. They were descendants of the Chanka, a rival tribe that fought with the Inca in the days of the empire. Once, in fact, the Chanka nearly conquered the Inca capital. Rómulo, Joshua and Ruben had heard Justiniano tell the tale many times.

The Chanka rose up against us in the days of Inca Urcu, eldest son of Inca Viracocha. They knew Urcu was a lazy drunkard, so when he sent the army off on a campaign, the Chanka attacked Cuzco.

But the Chanka had not taken into account the younger son of Inca Viracocha, Cusi Yupanqui, who had gone to war with the army. One night, God told Cusi in a dream about the siege. He immediately marched back to Cuzco. Cusi routed the Chanka, killing their king Asto Huaraca in hand-to-hand combat, and saved the city. The people of Cuzco made Cusi emperor in place of his worthless brother. When he ascended the throne, he changed his name from Cusi to Pachacutec. Inca Pachacutec became the greatest ruler of the empire. He gave the people wise laws and efficient government and urged them to worship the true God.

The Chanka suffered for their aggression. Pachacutec reduced them to vassals and forced many of them to leave their ancestral home to settle in distant parts of the empire. Because of this punishment, the Chanka hated the Inca more than ever. That was one reason why Huaman Inca Quicaña brought his family to Huamanga when he ran away from the Spanish. He knew the last place they would look for him was among his enemies, the Chanka. And that is also why, my sons, we have trouble with our Chanka neighbours even to this day.

Rómulo, Joshua and Ruben knew about the trouble their grandfather had with a Chanka neighbour when he was a young man, though Justiniano seldom told that story. The man's name was Huaranca and he lived in Culluhuanca, a Chanka village on the mountain slope above Chakiqpampa. A cattle rustler by vocation, Huaranca stole several horses from the Quicañas, who denounced the crime to local authorities. The authorities refused to take action, so Justiniano did. He tracked down the thief, caught him red-handed with the stolen animals and killed him.

Although he acted in self-defence, Justiniano later regretted his rash action. 'This happened long before I knew Jesus,' he explained to his grandsons. 'I would never have done anything so wrong as killing another man, had I known what the Bible teaches.'

'You must remember that the name "Inca" means "father of the poor",' he added. 'That means our family has a special responsibility here in Huamanga. We must set an example of justice and goodness for our neighbours, Chanka as well as

Inca. God expected this of Quicañas and Sauñes long before we were Christians. Now that we know Jesus, God expects even more of us.'

*   *   *

Rómulo, Joshua and Ruben knew well the story of how the Quicañas and Sauñes had become Christians. That was recent history. So recent, in fact, that the boys themselves were part of the story.

It began one stormy night in 1957 when Justiniano's brother-in-law Francisco Aviles brought two strangers to Justiniano's house in Chakiqpampa. 'Look, I've brought you a remedy,' Francisco said.

The whole clan had been looking for a remedy for Justiniano's drinking problem. The man consumed so much *chicha* and other kinds of liquor, that it scared his relatives. It even scared Justiniano. Teofila suffered the most from Justiniano's drinking. Her husband had developed a habit of beating his petite wife whenever he was under the influence.

'A remedy?' Justiniano asked, interested in seeing what Francisco had found this time to cure his alcoholism. 'What kind of remedy?'

Francisco showed Justiniano a New Testament the two men were carrying. 'This is the remedy,' he grinned. Francisco thought it a great joke. The two evangelists had shown up at his door on a rainy night, which obliged him to give them lodging. Francisco himself was in no mood to hear their talk of religion, however. That was why he had brought the men to Justiniano. 'They can't bother Justiniano, anyway,' he said to himself.'They don't speak Quechua and he knows no Spanish, so they won't be able to talk about religion.'

Despite the language barrier, the men did talk about religion to Justiniano and his family. They even read a verse from their New Testament. Justiniano's married daughter, Zoila, was staying at the house while her husband Enrique was away on business. Somehow, when she heard the words of John 3.16, 'for God so loved the world that he gave his only begotten son', she understood what they meant. That night Zoila believed in Jesus. Her mother Teofila and her 16-year-old brother Fernando believed, as well. As far as anyone knew, they were the first three people in the history of Chakiqpampa to be born again.

Justiniano Quicaña did not believe in Jesus that night. He continued to drink and beat Teofila. He also beat Zoila, now that she was an 'evangelical devil'. 'The catechist told us once that evangelicals grow horns and tails,' he told his daughter. 'Perhaps if I beat you enough, you won't grow a tail.' Justiniano was not the only person in Chakiqpampa to hold these views. When word got around that Teofila, Zoila and Fernando had professed faith in Christ, the new believers heard sneers of 'devils' and 'there go the demons' wherever they went.

'We'll kill these children of yours as we would kill frogs,' they taunted Zoila, pointing at little Rómulo and his sister Alejandrina. 'Better they die now than be raised by a devil.'

Zoila's problems worsened when Enrique returned from his business trip to learn that she had professed faith in Christ. He told her bluntly that she had gone to the devil. 'Those evangelicals are possessed by demons,' he said. 'You can see it in their eyes. They shine too brightly.'

'No, Enrique, it's not so,' she protested. 'You must surrender to Jesus, too. Then you will see for yourself.'

'You are mad!' he said. 'Here, drink this *chicha*. It will drive the demons out of you.'

Zoila refused. She also refused to chew the coca leaf that Enrique offered her. Nor would she go dancing with him in order to exorcise the gospel demon. 'All right then,' Enrique said, 'you live like this if you want, but not me. I'm leaving.' With that he disappeared, bound for Lima. Zoila would not see him again for two years. But his absence did not stop her from arising every day at 4.00 a.m. to pray for her husband's salvation.

Despite his initial rejection of the gospel, Justiniano Quicaña began to show signs of interest in the new faith. Perhaps he had understood more of the evangelists' message on that rainy evening than he admitted. Perhaps watching his wife and children stand firm in the face of persecution stirred him.

Maybe he only wanted a cure for his alcoholism. For whatever reason, or perhaps all three, Justiniano told Teofila that he wanted to find Jesus, too.'But I don't want to consult these goat skinner evangelists we have around here,' he said. 'I want to hear the Bible straight from the lips of a real missionary.'

To do that, he took Fernando and walked two days to Ayacucho to find Simon Izarra, a Quechua preacher his son had come to know. Justiniano managed to get himself stone drunk by the time they arrived at Izarra's house, where the preacher was leading a small worship service.

'Please, come back tomorrow when you're sober,' Izarra told Justiniano.'I'll be happy to talk with you then.'

'No sir, you've got to help me right now,' Justiniano insisted. 'Let's say I leave here, a truck runs over me and I die. What then? No, it has to be tonight, sir.'

Against his better judgement, Izarra led the tipsy Justiniano in a prayer of repentance and faith. Afterward, the man wobbled away into the night, leaning on his son's arm. That was the last inebriated night of Justiniano's life, however. Until his dying day he never tasted another drop of *chicha* or any other liquor. Nor did he ever again beat his wife. Justiniano Quicaña had found the remedy.

When his Quechua neighbours back in Chakiqpampa learned that Justiniano had professed faith in Christ, they began to greet him, too, with sneers of 'devil' wherever he went. The taunts intensified when Justiniano founded a Presbyterian church in his home. As far as anyone knew, it was the first evangelical congregation in the history of Chakiqpampa. However, Justiniano did not content himself with preaching the Bible merely in Chakiqpampa. He and Teofila toured surrounding communities – Culluhuanca, Andabamba, Ccahuiñayocc, Paccha and others – to tell Quechuas there about Jesus. The Quicañas even travelled to Huancavelica, Huanta, Huamanguilla and other points beyond Huamanga to tell Quechuas there about Jesus.

Their neighbours decided the Quicañas literally were going too far with their new faith. One night after returning from Huancavelica, Justiniano and Teofila faced a mob of drunken men bent on burning down their house. A mêlée ensued. It ended when petite Teofila took a tree limb to the side of one man's head, drawing blood. Another man, in his haste to retreat, fell into a gully and broke his leg. Next day, the district police summoned Teofila to their headquarters in Vinchos. Why had she mounted this unprovoked attack on her neighbours? they wanted to know. The police had been misinformed, she answered. She had acted in self-defence. Her neighbours were trying to burn down her house. Why would they want to do that? the police asked. Because the Quicañas had become evangelicals, Teofila answered. The police immediately knew she was telling the truth, because no one in rural Huamanga would claim to be an evangelical, unless she really were one. They dropped the assault charges against Teofila.

When Enrique Saúñe finally returned from Lima, he learned that most of his extended family, including his own parents, had become evangelicals. Lorenzo Saúñe was even preaching the Bible alongside Justiniano Quicaña. Still, Enrique would have nothing to do with Jesus. But his stubbornness did not stop Zoila from arising every day at 4.00 a.m. to pray for her husband's salvation.

One day Justiniano came to his son-in-law and thrust a wad of bills into his hands. 'Enrique, I want you to invest this money in cattle,' he said. 'You have been wandering about long enough trying to get rich. Use this capital to earn a decent living for your family.'

Enrique accepted Justiniano's money and went shopping for cattle. He found two young bulls for sale at a good price and bought them on the spot. A week later, two police officers arrived in Chakiqpampa. They had taken into custody the man from whom Enrique had purchased the bulls. They then arrested Enrique for buying stolen cattle. Because the rightful owner of the bulls lived in Huancavelica, the police jailed Enrique there, far from home.

While awaiting trial in the Huancavelica jail house, Enrique prayed to Jesus for the first time in his life. 'Lord Jesus, I know now that you do exist and I've done you great wrong. Forgive me, Lord, and help me get out of this prison.'

One night in a dream, Jesus answered him. Enrique saw himself lying in a dark, windowless house. He looked up to see two young men in bright robes removing tiles from the roof. Through the hole they dropped white cords down to Enrique. 'Tie these around your waist,' they directed. He did, and they drew him out into the bright light of freedom. Enrique turned to embrace his liberators but they were gone. He awoke from the dream, his face wet with tears.

Enrique found a New Testament that someone had placed among the few belongings he had brought from Chakiqpampa and started poring over its pages. Within days, he was preaching from that New Testament to the inmates in the prison yard. 'Listen, you devils,' he said with a wink to the few Christians there, 'I too have converted into a devil.' A sergeant saw Enrique preaching and sauntered over to him.

'Are you a brother?' the sergeant asked.

'Yes, sir.'

'Well, so am I,' the sergeant said, thrusting a second New Testament into Enrique's hands. 'Here, use this to preach to these thieves so that maybe they will give up thieving.'

A few days later, the sergeant took Enrique to the court house, where he was acquitted of the charges against him. Enrique left the Huancavelica jail house the same day, a free man.

Enrique knew God had sent him to prison for a reason. 'Here in Chakiqpampa, I was too carefree for the Lord to throw his lasso over me,' he told a friend. 'He had to take me to that corral in Huancavelica to catch me.'

Enrique was not an easy man to corral. A few weeks after returning home from jail, he told Zoila that God had called him to be a travelling evangelist. He was soon away on another business trip, the Lord's business. Zoila stayed home in Chakiqpampa to tend the family farm and raise her small children. In January 1962, during one of Enrique's frequent trips, she gave birth to another son, Joshua.

Enrique realized that it was not good to leave his family to go off alone preaching. He also decided the time had come for him to get proper training in the Bible. So he moved Zoila and the children to Ayacucho and enrolled in a Bible institute. After some study time in the city, Enrique decided he needed to preach the gospel to Quechuas migrating to the lower Apurimac basin. There homesteaders were clearing tropical forests and planting oranges, bananas and coca leaf. Enrique moved his family into a grass shack in the jungle. They did not live there long. Zoila and the children suffered from torrid heat and swarming insects and Enrique failed to find suitable work to support them. The family moved back to Ayacucho.

Settling in the city proved to be a major turning point in young Rómulo Sauñe's life. Instead of pasturing sheep and goats all day, he now went to school. Not that school was necessarily more pleasant than shepherding, especially for a small boy who spoke no Spanish. Rómulo was further handicapped by a chronic hearing problem he had developed in Chakiqpampa after being kicked in the head by a horse. His early teachers dismissed him as another 'stupid' Quechua boy with no aptitude for letters.

Rómulo Sauñe did have aptitude for letters, however. Exceptional aptitude, not just for letters, but for linguistics. Rómulo Sauñe, in fact, would grow up to become a professional linguist. This came about after studies of communications and theology in the United States, which came after Rómulo, at age 15, prayed with Simon Izarra to receive Christ, just as his parents and grandparents had done. One day, like his parents and grandparents, Rómulo would preach the Bible to his Quechua neighbours in rural Huamanga. In fact, one day Rómulo would translate the Bible into Quechua for his neighbours in rural Huamanga.

*   *   *

The move to Ayacucho meant that Joshua Sauñe would also go to school. Like his elder brother Rómulo, Joshua would learn to speak Spanish and to read and write. But Joshua did not lose contact with his Quechua roots. The stories he had heard from Justiniano Quicaña burned in his heart and mind. Joshua believed his Inca heritage bequeathed to him a duty to help his people. Joshua would strive to set an example of goodness and justice for his Quechua neighbours, just as God expected of him.

Joshua began striving for justice for the Quechuas while still in school, in fact. Once, he learned that some city boys were stealing money from a poor Quechua woman who sold sweets on the sidewalk outside the school. Joshua tracked down the thieves, retrieved the money and returned it to its rightful owner. To help him, Joshua recruited his younger brother Ruben and his best friend, Carlos Trisollini. Carlos was part Italian, as his father's surname indicated, but his mother was full Quechua. His lineage instilled in Carlos the same loyalties to the Quechua people that the Sauñe brothers felt. The three boys even made a blood pact: if any one of them were hurt or killed, the other two would exact vengeance.

As he got older, Joshua heard other voices talk about justice for his people. Shining Path cadres appeared in Ayacucho, first at the National University of San Cristobal of Huamanga and then in humble neighbourhoods of the working class, like the one where the Sauñes lived. 'Come, help us work for justice,' they bade Joshua. 'We have the same goals as you: to take wealth from the corrupt rich and redistribute it to the working-class poor.'

Shining Path propaganda did not attract Joshua in the least. He did not need their particular brand of ideology to justify taking from the rich to give to the poor. In the 1970s, drug traffickers had begun operating in Peru. By then, thousands of Quechuas had migrated to the lower Apurimac basin to grow coca leaf, which they sold to the traffickers. The traffickers processed the leaf into cocaine paste, which they sold, at a huge profit, to Colombian drug cartels. The cartels refined the paste into powder for sale, at yet greater profit, to consumers in the United States and Europe. The Quechua farmers who worked hard raising coca leaf in the torrid jungles did not see these huge profits, and this angered Joshua. It angered him even more when the traffickers began selling cocaine paste, *pichicata* as it was known locally, to Ayacucho youth, teaching them how to smoke it in hand-rolled cigarettes. Many youths, even Quechua youth, had become addicted to *pichicata*. Joshua determined he would right this wrong by stealing the drug traffickers' ill-gotten wealth and distributing it among the poor of his people. He did not think this improper. In fact, he would be doing God's work, just as his grandfather had taught him.

Joshua was 17 when he organized his first raid. He and his gang surprised a band of traffickers at a small *pichicata* factory in the lower Apurimac basin. After tying up the traffickers at gunpoint, the boys dumped their stock of cocaine paste into the river and stole a rucksack full of cash. The rucksack contained US$50,000, which Joshua gave away to poor Quechua widows and the elderly homeless.

Just before his eighteenth birthday, Joshua organized a second raid. This one required his gang to spend a week in the jungle, watching the movements of a band of traffickers at a large *pichicata* factory. When they determined all was ready, they surprised the traffickers, tied them up at gunpoint, dumped their stock of cocaine paste into the river and stole three rucksacks full of cash. Joshua knew these rucksacks contained much more than US$50,000; however, he never got a chance to count the money.

The day following the raid, the boys arrived at the banks of the Apurimac. Spent from a week of sleepless nights and a day of lugging heavy money sacks through the jungle, they stopped to rest. Joshua took off his boots to find out why they made a squishing sound with every step and saw it was because they had filled with blood oozing from the blisters on his feet. He was examining the blisters when bullets began slamming into the river bank around him.

Unknown to the boys, one of the traffickers had slipped his bonds, untied his companions and alerted nearby *pichicata* factories about the raid. A band of well-armed traffickers had pursued the boys all night and caught up with them when they stopped to rest. Joshua dived behind a boulder and returned the fire, allowing his companions to escape across the river. But his ammunition ran out and Joshua had to surrender. He stood on the beach with his hands in the air as a man walked up to him, loaded two shells in the handsome shotgun he carried, pointed it at Joshua's chest, and pulled the trigger, twice. The gun failed to fire. In the stunned silence that followed, Joshua saw a vision of his father, mother and brothers weeping over his dead body. The sight prompted the boy to dive into the river and try swimming away. The traffickers sent a powerboat after him, which circled the lad several times until he had swallowed so much of the wake water he knew he was drowning. He had to surrender again. This time they chained him to a tree and discussed what to do. Joshua saw the men unsheathing machetes and overheard someone say, 'Let's cut him up and feed him to the fish.'

They likely would have done so, had not one of men come up to Joshua, peered into his face and asked: 'Aren't you the son of Enrique Sauñe?'

'Yes, I am.'

The man shook his head ruefully and said to his companions, 'We can't kill this boy. I know his father. He used to come around here preaching the gospel.'

The men talked it over and decided the best option would be to turn the boy over to the authorities. They delivered Joshua to the police in a nearby town, who arrested him on charges of attempted robbery, which he had committed, and drug trafficking, which, of course, he had not. The court sentenced him to 15 years in prison, a much more lenient sentence than his captors would have given him had they never heard his father preach the gospel.

Unlike his elder brother Rómulo, Joshua had never prayed with Simon Izarra to receive Christ. In fact, Joshua did not pray to Jesus until a year after arriving in San Miguel prison. It happened late one night, after a failed escape attempt left Joshua depressed and desperate.

I was taking out my anger on God that night when I had a vision. I saw a person – but I couldn't look at his face, it was very, very bright – who came through the door where we were sleeping. He told me that if I wanted to be free of that prison, I had to follow him. I said, 'Lord, who are you?' He said, 'Jesus.' He took a scroll from under his arm and in it was written – in blue letters, I remember it well – everything

I had ever done. He said, 'If you want to be forgiven of these things, then follow me.'

Tears started to roll down my cheeks. All I could say was, 'Lord, thank you, thank you.' But he disappeared. I thought I was losing my mind. I said, 'Lord Jesus, if you really do exist, give me proof. If Papa comes to see me tomorrow, I will follow you. I won't escape. I'll be here until you free me from this jail.'

Joshua thought he was making a safe wager. Enrique Sauñe had not visited his son for several weeks. When he did not show up by noon the following day, the hour when the last bus from Ayacucho arrived at the prison, Joshua felt greatly relieved. Jesus did not exist, after all, he assured himself. He had only been dreaming last night and he need not keep the foolish promise he made to God. The boy was feeling almost jovial by mid-afternoon when the guard called him.

'Sauñe, you have a visitor.'

Joshua was trembling when he reached the door and saw his father standing there. Enrique looked his son over from head to toe before speaking. 'Are you okay?'

'Yes, Papa, I'm fine,' he said weakly.

'Joshua, you know we are very busy this time of year. That's why we haven't been to see you. Sorry about it.' He paused briefly. 'Well, last night your mother had a dream and thought something had happened to you. She's been begging me all morning to come see you. I started late and missed the last bus. I was on my way back home when a fellow came by in a pickup, asked if I were going to San Miguel and told me to get in. Funny thing, but after he let me out, I turned to thank him and he had disappeared.'

Joshua stared mutely at this father, but he was thinking: God really does exist and he cares about me. He told Jesus, 'Lord, I am going to follow you just as my brothers follow you, just as my grandparents and parents follow you. I will not turn back.'

Joshua kept his promise and so did Jesus. A year later, Joshua left San Miguel prison, acquitted of all criminal charges

against him. At the first opportunity, he went to see his grandfather, Justiniano Quicaña.

He found the old man sitting on a great boulder on the
slopes above Chakiqpampa while his livestock grazed about
him. Justiniano wept when he saw his grandson. It was the
only time, Joshua would later recall, he ever saw his grandfather weep. Justiniano embraced the boy and they sat together
on the rock.

'Joshua, you are suffering much,' the old man said. 'It's
because you were born to suffer. It is your destiny to lead our
people.'

The comment startled Joshua. 'Grandfather, I don't understand,' he said

'I was the one who named you "Joshua", which means "God
with us". Did you know I was with your mother when you
were born? You thrust out your hands first, grasping about to
pull yourself from the womb. When I saw that, I said, "Here is
a man to lead the Quechuas." So I gave you the name Joshua,
who was leader of the Israelites.'

Justiniano sighed. 'But your fault has been to go about it in
the wrong way, Joshua. From now on, you must lead our people by the Word of God. If you will do that, then you will see
that God truly is with you.'

That afternoon they spent together would be their last.
Soon afterward, Joshua would leave for the United States to
attend Bible college. This was on the advice of his elder brother
Rómulo, who had recently returned from studies in California.
Bible school was not Joshua's idea, however. Immediately after
completing the three-year course, he would study art for two
years in Arizona. There he would become a successful artist,
marry and not return to Peru for many years. By then, Justiniano
Quicaña would be gone.

Nevertheless, the words that his grandfather spoke to him
that afternoon on the slopes above Chakiqpampa burned in
Joshua Sauñe's heart.

3

The Beginnings of
Peace and Hope

Odd though it sounds, Peace and Hope greatly increased following the 1984 murder of six Christian men of the Presbyterian Church in Callqui at the hands of Marine Infantry of the Peruvian Navy.

Callqui is a village a mile above the provincial capital of Huanta, which lies an hour's journey north of Ayacucho. Shining Path cadres from the National University of San Cristobal of Huamanga infiltrated the area around Huanta in the late 1970s, seeking to recruit peasant farmers to the revolution. Initially, they met with some success, largely due to discontent with the military dictatorship that governed Peru in those years. As is true with most military dictatorships, the government did not tolerate dissent. In one tragic incident, high school students in Huanta staged a public march to protest against a rise in school fees. Police fired on the crowd, killing 21 of the marchers. On each subsequent anniversary of the protest, local residents commemorated the young martyrs with a public march. Tension between Huanta and the military government intensified. When young *senderistas* appeared and began talking about a popular uprising that would overthrow the dictators, eradicate poverty and usher in social equality, some of the local residents signed on as supporters.

Discontent among local residents intensified at the outset of 1983, when the government, now headed by civilian politicians, deployed marines in the Huanta area to fight Shining Path. The infantrymen, most of whom were middle-class youth from the city, had little understanding of or respect for the

Quechuas in the peasant communities around Huanta. Because the Path had recruited some of these peasant farmers to their cause, the marines tended to suspect all Quechuas of being Shining Path supporters. To keep them from aiding the revolution, military units torched the farmers' homes and fields and confiscated their livestock, which they either butchered to supplement their diet or sold to supplement their pay.

Heavy-handed military repression helped the Path recruit yet more peasant farmers to their cause. In fact, some signed on as Shining Path supporters simply to protect themselves from the marines. They had no illusions about eradicating poverty or ushering in social equality, they only wanted to survive.

Had Shining Path known better how to exploit discontent, it might well have succeeded in defeating the marines. But instead, the Path tended to drive supporters away from its cause as fast as they recruited them. The problem was that the *senderistas*, many of whom were middle-class youth from the city, treated the Quechuas with little respect or understanding. In this, they resembled the marines.

The *senderistas'* first mistake arose from their lack of historical understanding. In 'liberated' communities under control of the Path, revolutionary cadres insisted on reorganizing farm land into communist collectives. This was just after Peru had implemented sweeping agrarian reform intended to right a historic wrong. At the time of the Spanish conquest, land that had belonged to the Inca empire was taken from the Quechuas by the Europeans, who forced them to farm their holdings as indentured tenants. As happened with medieval feudalism in Europe, the landlords got rich while the tenant farmers sank deeper and deeper into poverty. This modified feudal system survived, more or less intact, for nearly 500 years. Then in the 1970s, the government of Peru transferred land from the hands of wealthy landlords to their tenant farmers. Quechuas once again controlled land that had belonged to their ancestors centuries before. Then the Path came along and told them they must turn their land over to the revolution. The idea did not catch on quickly.

The *senderistas'* second mistake arose from a lack of social understanding. They insisted that women, as well as men, work the land. This was necessary in order to produce a surplus of crops, which went to feed guerrilla battalions. The idea made perfect sense to the middle-class youth of the Path who knew nothing about farming, but it struck the Quechuas as loathsome. 'Even the landlords never forced our *women* to work in the fields,' they protested. The complaints of village leaders availed little to change the policies of Shining Path. In fact, the Path grew more and more impatient with leaders of rural Quechua communities and finally decided to replace them with persons of its own choosing. In the latter half of 1982, Presidente Gonzalo ordered the abolition of all municipal governments in liberated zones under the Path's control. From that time on, 'people's committees' designated by guerrilla commanders were to govern Quechua villages. This was another tragic mistake.

The *senderistas'* lack of political understanding caused this error. The Quechua system of traditional leadership dated from the time of their Inca forebears. It was a basic element of their culture. When Quechuas talk of 'town fathers', that is exactly what they understand their leaders to be. Neither Spanish conqueror nor European landlord had ever dared replace town fathers with leaders of their own choosing. When the Quechuas learned of this decision, they were appalled. The *senderistas* listened to peasant protests against the policy, but were not dissuaded. They had their orders, from Presidente Gonzalo himself. His decree was part of the 'Second Grand Plan of Deployment in the War of all Wars' and could not be rescinded.

Town fathers who refused to abandon their posts – and there were a great many in the Quechua communities around Huanta – faced assassination at the hands of the Path. Some died in ambushes on deserted paths or isolated mountain roads. Some were kidnapped, subjected to 're-education' and then killed if they did not capitulate to the new order. Sometimes, Shining Path cadres invaded disobedient communities and staged 'people's trials' in the village plaza.

The *senderistas* often condemned town fathers as 'enemies of the revolution' and cut their throats or strangled them as horrified neighbours watched. The intent of such public executions was to eliminate troublesome leaders while intimidating Quechua communities into submission. They invariably produced the opposite effect.

The marines might have won their war against terrorism early on, had they exploited the Path's mistakes. Once the *senderistas* began killing town fathers, Quechua communities would gladly have helped the marines rid the country of the terrorists. But unfortunately the marines made mistakes of their own. The first was to assume that the Quechua peasants around Huanta cooperated with the *senderistas* because they chose to do so, rather than because they feared retaliation if they did not. Heedless of these particulars, military commanders delivered swift and fierce punishment on any Quechuas who cooperated with the Path. Marines torched their homes and fields, then hauled them off to jail. There, interrogators tortured them to extract information. Afterwards, they executed them and disposed of their bodies. Officially, the dead were listed as 'disappeared'. Eventually, the marines did not bother to 'disappear' Shining Path collaborators after arrest and interrogation. They simply executed them on the spot.

That is how the six Christian men in Callqui died. It was a Wednesday evening and a few believers had gathered at the Presbyterian church, as was their custom, for prayer. Someone informed the nearby Marine Infantry base of the meeting, which was technically illegal because of a ban on public gatherings around Huanta. When the marines arrived, they searched the church building for evidence linking the believers to the Path. They found two wooden rifles stored in a closet. Everyone recognized such toy guns as patriotic symbols. Boys carried the wooden rifles in civic parades to show their loyalty to Peru and their willingness to defend their country. The marines did not recognize them as such, however, insisting the wooden rifles were used to train terrorists, which meant that the Presbyterian church was, in reality, a terrorist training base. The marines ordered the six men attending the prayer meeting to go outside and lie on the ground. They obeyed. One of the marines stayed behind to stand guard at the church door. 'Keep singing,' he ordered the remaining worshippers. The terrified women and children obeyed. Machine-gun fire suddenly interrupted the hymns. A moment later, a grenade exploded against the front wall of the church. Then all was quiet. The marines had gone. The handful of believers stole out to the church yard and found the mutilated and blood-soaked bodies of the six men. The marines had made another tragic mistake.

*   *   *

Whether committed by the Path or the marines, the atrocities of the early 1980s visited unthinkable terror on the peasant farmers in Huanta, Huamanga and other rural provinces in the department of Ayacucho. Indeed, in this war it seemed Shining Path and their military adversaries were less interested in killing each other than in killing innocent civilians caught between the battle lines. Cases were reported of villages invaded by strangers who said they were *senderistas*. They demanded food. When the peasants served them, the strangers threw off their disguises to reveal themselves as soldiers. The unsuspecting farmers who fed them were either disappeared or executed on the spot. Some *senderistas* learned of this nefarious tactic and adopted it as well, posing as military troops and asking peasants for information about terrorist incursions. If the farmers gave the information, the terrorists declared them 'enemies of the revolution' and cut their throats. Quechua peasants learned to mistrust strangers.

Mistrust was but one product of the terror. Disrespect for the dead was another. The Path was to blame for introducing this particular barbarity. The *senderistas* began dumping the corpses of its victims in public places, say, a park or roadway, with signs clearly identifying the deceased as enemies of the revolution. Informants would watch to see who collected the body for burial. The Path identified those persons – whether family or friend of the deceased or simply decent citizens – as enemies of the revolution and marked them for elimination. Military and police officers eventually adopted the tactic. The corpses of 'disappeared' persons began turning up alongside roadways and other public places. 'Those are terrorists,' they warned passers-by. Whether family, friend or simply decent citizen, nobody dared touch the bodies.

As a result, the countryside of Huanta, Huamanga and other provinces around Ayacucho became littered with the unburied corpses of victims of the violence. Ayacuchans dreaded trips over rural roadways, knowing they would see carrion birds circling dead bodies left in the open to rot. Some, like Ismael Garcia, witnessed worse barbarity. Ismael, the father-in-law of Demetrio Sauñe, arose one morning and stepped out of his front door to see his dogs gnawing on two human heads.

Ismael lived on the edge of a deep ravine near Ocros, a village in rural Huamanga where the Marine Infantry maintained a base. Scores of *senderista* collaborators were jailed in the stockade in Ocros for interrogation. One night, the soldiers selected 72 of their prisoners for disappearance. These were loaded on a truck, driven to the deep ravine outside town and lined up on the edge. The marines executed the suspects with machine guns. Their bodies fell into the ravine and were left unburied. If any passers-by found them there, none dared touch the corpses. None, of course, except the carrion birds and Ismael Garcia's dogs.

It is said that the first casualty in every war is human rights. That was certainly the case in Peru during the Shining Path war. Peruvians, especially those living in the rural provinces of the department of Ayacucho, lost most of the rights that mark us as human beings. Decent citizens lost the right to live in peace and security. The accused lost the right to a fair and impartial trial. Even the dead lost the right to rest in peace. Human rights suffered terribly in the terrorist war. That was why Peru so desperately needed Peace and Hope.

*   *   *

Pedro Arana served as founding chairman of the Peace and Hope Commission while he also served as vice-president of the National Council of Evangelicals of Peru, CONEP, as it is known by its Spanish acronym. Arana is the only man alive who signed both of two historic documents. The first is the charter of the Latin American branch of the International Fellowship of Evangelical Students, which Arana and several other university students from around the continent organized in 1958. The second historic document was the Constitution of 1979 of the Republic of Peru, which Arana, as a deputy to the National Constituent Assembly, helped draft. Between those two landmarks in his life, Arana earned a degree in chemical engineering from San Marcos University in Lima and a degree in theology from Free College, Edinburgh, Scotland. Meanwhile he pastored Presbyterian churches and immersed himself in the public affairs of Peru.

The deplorable state of public affairs brought on by the terrorist war prompted CONEP to organize the Peace and Hope Commission in 1984. The Commission's primary task was to provide food, clothing and medicine to the thousands of refugees fleeing the violence in the department of Ayacucho. Great urgency attended this task. Yet when the six Presbyterian men in Callqui died at the hands of the Marine Infantry, Peace and Hope found itself immersed in another urgent task: defending human rights. Great danger attended this task.

Vicente Saico, the director of a Christian radio station in Huanta, learned of the Callqui murders from terrified Presbyterian believers who came to his home in the early hours of the morning following the massacre. Saico, who spoke Quechua as they did, was the first person the witnesses thought to contact. It was good they did. Saico helped them arrange for a proper police investigation of the crime scene, which produced forensic evidence that corroborated the witnesses' account of the slayings. Saico then broadcast news of the murders over the radio and wrote a letter to CONEP officials informing them of the incident. The public exposure ensured that the murderers would not visit the Presbyterian church a second time to try to cover up their crime. The murderers, however, did attempt a cover-up. Jaime Ayala, a journalist who reported the Callqui murders in the local newspaper, naming the marine patrol responsible and their commanding officer, disappeared without a trace.

The week after the Callqui murders, CONEP president Miguel Angel Palomino came to Ayacucho along with Pedro Arana and Tito Paredes, who served with Arana on the Peace and Hope Commission. The three men planned to meet with Vicente Saico and some 30 local pastors to discuss the Callqui case and what CONEP could do about it. When they arrived, the three visitors found 300 fellow Christians awaiting them. Many of these were present due to the public exposure of the Callqui murders. Many more had come to see what CONEP could do about the violence in their own communities.

As a result of that meeting, three things happened within the National Council of Evangelicals of Peru. One, its leadership recognized that no sincere Christian could stand idly by while fellow believers suffered looting, rape and murder. Henceforth, CONEP would publicly expose such atrocities, whether committed in the name of the revolution or in the name of the state. Second, CONEP committed itself to defending human rights as part of the working agenda of the Peace and Hope Commission. Third, Pedro Arana would resign as pastor of the Pueblo Libre Presbyterian Church and devote all his time and energy to Peace and Hope.

*   *   *

Vicente Saico faced great danger because of his role in exposing the Callqui murderers. His daughter Janeth remembers the time he awakened her and her five brothers and sisters in the middle of the night. 'The marines are outside in the street,' he told them softly. Janeth looked out her window to see a line of hooded soldiers, machine guns at the ready, lined up on the opposite pavement.

'Please, everyone get out of bed and go to the back room to pray,' Vicente instructed his family. 'We must ask for God's protection.'

As the Saico family prayed, the marines acted. They broke through the door and rushed into . . . the house next door. It was a clear case of mistaken intelligence. The Saicos' neighbour was a handicapped man confined to a wheelchair. The marines could find absolutely no evidence linking him to

Shining Path. Their only option was to withdraw. Thankfully, no one disappeared that night.

Despite their narrow escape, Vicente Saico knew his family could expect more unwelcome visits from both soldiers and *senderistas*. Broadcasters were frequent targets of the Path, who kidnapped radio technicians and forced them to serve the communication needs of the revolution. Broadcasters with families were at special risk. The Path held their loved ones hostage to ensure that the radio technicians obeyed orders. That December when school finished, Vicente told the family they would be spending the holidays in Lima. The holiday stretched into a year and a half. The Saicos did not return home until 1986, in fact, the year the government withdrew the Marine Infantry from Huanta.

Pedro Arana also faced great danger for his role in exposing the Callqui murderers. On the first anniversary of the massacre, he published a stinging condemnation of the crime in the *Peace and Hope Bulletin*. 'Apart from the shedding of innocent blood of these six believers,' he wrote, 'a humble sanctuary was desecrated and He whose glory and majesty cannot be contained in any cathedral was treated with contempt.'

The public outcry against the Callqui murders obliged the Navy to bring a court-martial against Captain Alvaro Artaza, the marine officer who ordered the killings. A military tribunal heard arguments for the defence. Initially, Artaza alleged that perhaps the murderers were not marines at all, but *senderistas* disguised in military uniforms. That argument faltered on the positive identification of the witnesses and the spent shell casings that police found at the crime scene. The casings matched marine weapons perfectly. Next, the defence argued that the Callqui Presbyterians were 'linked, according to our suspicions, to the subversion'. Artaza supported this argument by citing the two wooden rifles stored in the church closet. Although he failed to explain why this suspicion justified his order to shoot six men in cold blood while they lay defenceless on the ground, the tribunal accepted the argument. Judges postponed a verdict, pending further deliberations.

Even if the tribunal had returned a guilty verdict against

Artaza, the stiffest sentence given him, under military law, would have been a 'severe reprimand'. Military regulations granted officers *de facto* impunity for crimes committed in the line of duty. Impunity, in turn, led to atrocities like those committed in Callqui and Ocros and scores of other rural communities in the department of Ayacucho. CONEP leaders concluded that, should Captain Artaza be cleared of responsibility in the Callqui murders, human rights would continue to be a tragic casualty of the terrorist war.

Their conclusion prompted CONEP, acting as legal counsel for the Presbyterian Church, to petition civilian prosecutors to bring homicide charges against Alvaro Artaza. In his capacity as chairman of the Peace and Hope Commission, Pedro Arana was appointed to oversee the legal proceedings. From the start, Arana ran into massive obstacles. For one, few lawyers were willing to take on the powerful Peruvian military, especially the few lawyers whose fees CONEP could afford. So Arana enlisted the services of a 24-year-old law student in his final year of university.

José Regalado would not have been much help to Arana and the Peace and Hope Commission during his first years of university, to be sure. At that time, by his own account, the young man was an atheist who dabbled in the teachings of Marx and rated Christians in the same class as extra-terrestrials – odd sorts who confused myth with reality. One day at law school, José got hold of a copy of *Jesus the Great Radical*, a paper published by the local branch of the International Fellowship of Evangelical Students. The paper captivated the young law student for its penetrating analysis of the human condition, especially the human condition in Peru. José began having conversations with campus Christians about life, faith and the gospel. They introduced him to the Scriptures, which captivated him yet further. José grew more and more convinced that what the Bible said was true, even as he grew more and more disillusioned with communist ideology. He came to the startling conclusion that it was he, not the Christians, who had confused myth with reality. One day on campus, José confessed Jesus as Lord. He accepted baptism, joined the Christian and

Missionary Alliance Church and became active in the local branch of the Fellowship of Evangelical Students.

It was there José met Pedro Arana and agreed to help him with the legal proceedings against Alvaro Artaza. Regalado began marshalling evidence and writing arguments to convince the civil courts to try the captain for the Callqui murders. Regalado was not the only legal counsel Arana consulted. He had several lawyer friends within the political community, thanks to his participation in the constituent assembly of 1979. But the attorneys could offer Arana little more than advice on the matter, since CONEP could not afford their fees. Finances were the least of Arana's worries, however. Peru's powerful politicians staunchly supported the military. That fact became evident when Fernando Belaúnde Terry, the President of Peru, was asked to comment on the homicide charges CONEP leaders sought to bring against Alvaro Artaza. 'The people who are accusing the powerful armed forces of our country had better take heed,' he said.

Peruvians had learned to take such statements seriously. Veiled threats from powerful politicians often translated into night-time raids and disappeared persons. Rosemary Palomino, Emma Arana and Joy Paredes, the wives of the three CONEP leaders who were most directly involved in the Callqui case, gathered regularly to pray for their husbands' safety. 'If they are to die in this cause, then they must die,' they prayed. 'Nevertheless, we would like to have them alive, Lord, so let thy will be done.' As it turned out, Rosemary Palomino herself played a part in the answer to those prayers. One day, Mrs Palomino met a general in the Air Force to arrange for military transport of food, clothing and medicines that Peace and Hope was sending to refugees in Ayacucho. In the course of the conversation, she mentioned the Callqui case and the danger it represented for her husband and other CONEP leaders. The general agreed to meet Pedro Arana and hear his side of the story. After doing so, the officer, who commanded Air Force intelligence, assured the Peace and Hope chairman that he was doing the right thing and promised to speak on his behalf to his colleagues in the high command. The general kept his word and Arana, Palomino and Paredes received no night-time visits from the powerful armed forces of their country.

On the other hand, Peace and Hope did not receive a fair and impartial hearing of its case against the Callqui murderers either. Military courts delayed action against Alvaro Artaza for more than a year, then transferred the case from the Ayacucho jurisdiction to Lima. In June 1986, a military tribunal there ordered the case closed, in effect declaring Artaza and his marines acquitted of the murder charges. CONEP appealed to the Supreme Court, presenting the evidence José Regalado and other lawyers had prepared. The Supreme Court, in an unprecedented show of indifference, declined to hear the case. The decision of the military tribunal would stand.

Public outcry against the miscarriage of justice in the Callqui case translated into yet another disappeared person. Three days after the Supreme Court decision, Alvaro Artaza went missing. Military spokesmen claimed he had been kidnapped by Shining Path terrorists and even released the names of suspects. Several weeks passed with no more news about the captain's whereabouts, a curious thing, given the fact that the security forces supposedly knew who had abducted him. Military officers declined to comment on the matter, and eventually the public outcry diminished. Artaza evidently survived his kidnapping ordeal. He later turned up as military attaché to the Peruvian embassy in Panama. The terrorist war had once again claimed human rights as a casualty.

The Callqui affair claimed one more casualty – Pedro Arana. The founding chairman of the Peace and Hope Commission agonized over the failure of his organization to win justice for the Callqui martyrs. In December 1986, Arana felt compelled to resign 'in the interests of harmony'. He later took an administrative post with the Christian relief agency World Vision. Caleb Meza, a sociologist and lay pastor of the Evangelical Church in Peru, took over leadership of Peace and Hope.

Yet, the Callqui affair did not end in complete failure. Due to the public outcry over the case, international human rights groups stepped up efforts to monitor abuses committed by both the military and Shining Path. Americas Watch and

Amnesty International conducted inquiries into the Callqui murders. The latter organization reported: 'Protest in Peru against the participation of the Marine Infantry in cases of disappearances and political homicides increased, following the August 1984 report of a marine patrol that shot to death six religious leaders in front of the Evangelical Presbyterian Church of Callqui.' Peruvians learned to take such protests seriously. Protest, in fact, began saving lives. Human rights monitors reported a 75 per cent *decline* in civilian deaths in the terrorist war after 1984.

Odd though it sounds, the Callqui case also served to bring Christians in Peru closer together. In September 1984, Monsignor Javier Ariz, the Auxiliar Bishop of Lima, set a historical precedent by sending a personal letter to CONEP leaders. On behalf of ranking members of the Roman Catholic clergy, Ariz expressed his 'profound condolences for the violent deaths of the members of the Presbyterian Church of Callqui'. Ariz also asked CONEP leaders to convey 'to the brothers of the Presbyterian Church of Callqui, the testimony of our pain, along with our most energetic protest against these acts, which are shedding so much blood and exacerbating the differences between brothers'. Eventually Roman Catholics, who until that time had no official relationship with Protestants, would be working alongside evangelical Christians to fight for peace and justice in Peru.

Christians in other parts of the world also began working for peace and justice in Peru. Vicente Saico received a letter from Swiss-based Christian Solidarity International expressing the organization's condemnation for the attack on the Callqui church. President Fernando Belaúnde also received a letter from Christian Solidarity International, calling for an investigation into the matter. Presbyterians from Scotland to Canada sent similar letters to Peru, along with donations to the Peace and Hope Commission to provide food, clothing and medicines to refugees. Donations arrived from organizations such as the Swiss Mission, Latin Link and Tearfund. The latter organization would continue its donations for several years, helping to underwrite the efforts of the Peace and Hope Commission in defending human rights.

A final outcome of the Callqui case was to give a 24-year-old law school student experience in defending human rights. Following his graduation, José Regalado left Peace and Hope for a period of two years to establish himself in private law practice. He needed a steady income to support his new wife, Ruth Alvarado, whom he met through the Fellowship of Evangelical Students and married in March 1987. He would later return to work with Peace and Hope. But this time round, things would be different. For one thing, José would be working alongside a full team of Christian activists that Caleb Meza had recruited to the cause of defending human rights. The other difference: this time, Peace and Hope would win.

4

The Ashaninka

At the close of the nineteenth century, when great numbers of highlanders began migrating to the central jungles of Peru, they nicknamed the natives they found living there *campas*. Anthropologists say the epithet is derived from the Quechua word *thampa*, which means 'ragged'. Possibly the highlanders used this term for the natives because of the coarse, hand-made tunics they wore. Nevertheless, the natives do not like outsiders to call them *campas*. In their own tongue, they refer to themselves as *Ashaninka*, which is 'the people'. Anthropologists say the term literally means 'we people' as opposed to the *atsiri*, which means 'everybody else'.

For most of their history, the Ashaninka have got along tolerably well with everybody else. The first outsiders to arrive in the lush, low foothills of the Andes where the 25,000 Ashaninka make their home were Franciscan missionaries who established outposts on the Ene, Tambo and upper Ucayali Rivers early in the eighteenth century. Except for the occasional adventurer, few other highlanders entered the jungles over the next two centuries, kept at bay by mosquitoes, malaria and the natives' well-deserved reputation as adept warriors. The Ashaninka lived relatively unmolested in their fertile foothills, hunting, fishing and growing manioc, yams, bananas and peanuts.

Around the turn of the twentieth century, world demand for rubber, coffee and cocoa surged. Outsiders poured into the jungle, seeking their fortunes. The Ashaninka lost hundreds of thousands of hectares of their foothills to the *atsiri*, particularly in the upper reaches of the Rivers. Some of the migrants hired Ashaninkas to work in tropical agribusiness. Some of these employers coveted fortune so much they virtually enslaved the natives, paying abysmal wages for long days spent gathering rubber or tending coffee and cocoa trees. As a result, many of the Ashaninka learned to work for themselves, planting coffee and cocoa to feed world demand for those products, and rice and beans to feed the migrants. But they did not covet fortune as the outsiders did. They wanted only to feed their families and live in peace with everybody else. For despite their well-deserved reputation as adept warriors, the Ashaninka prefer not to start fights.

Some of the outsiders did start fights, however. In 1965, a group known as the Movement of the Revolutionary Left staged an armed uprising against the government. Two Revolutionary Left leaders, Guillermo Lobatón and Máximo Velando, organized a guerrilla army in the central jungle. Not long into the campaign, government troops captured Velando and the short-lived rebellion ended. Nonetheless, the uprising had caused undeserved trouble for the Ashaninka, for although they did not start the fight, some of them died in it.

Around the middle of the twentieth century, a second wave of Christian missionaries, comprised almost entirely of evangelical Protestants, began arriving in the central jungle. In 1947, Sylvester and Matilda Dirks from the Mennonite Brethren Church of Canada settled on the Tambo River and started teaching the Scriptures to the Ashaninka. In 1950, linguists of the Wycliffe Bible Translators arrived on the upper reaches of the Ene River and commenced translating the Scriptures into the Ashaninka language. Some Ashaninka soon professed faith in Christ. The new believers began to form churches and more evangelical missionaries arrived.

Paul Friesen, tall and lean with piercing blue eyes, looks more like a rugged cowboy from Kansas, where he grew up, than a Bible professor from the central jungle, where he has spent the past 40 years of his life. Friesen and his wife Maurine first arrived in Peru on Valentine's Day 1960. The couple took up residence near the town of Atalaya, where the Tambo River meets the Ucayali. Missionaries had built an airstrip there. Paul eventually learned Ashaninka well enough to teach theology and serve as consultant to linguists who were translating

Scriptures. Meanwhile, he wrote a textbook in Spanish on the Gospel of Mark. Maurine advised the natives on how to market their beans and rice to river traders and helped them market their peanuts, mainly as butter, to Wycliffe bush pilots who stopped in Atalaya to refuel their aircraft. In the meantime, she raised the five Friesen children.

Missionary colleagues of the Friesens taught other skills to the Ashaninka. Some trained native midwives to deliver babies and administer injections. Others advised tribal leaders on how to negotiate the complex Peruvian justice system in order to secure legal title to their lands. Some taught the natives how to become teachers themselves. Soon the tribe began to form its own bilingual schools to educate their children in Ashaninka and Spanish.

During the 1970s, the missionaries advised the Ashaninka on how to strengthen the schools and churches they had formed. Tribal leaders negotiated with the government to gain accreditation for Ashaninka schools and grant salaries for bilingual teachers. In effect, the tribe created its own school system. The school system, in turn, began to modify the tribal lifestyle. Until then, the Ashaninka had been semi-nomadic people, living in small family clans loosely dispersed throughout the lush foothills. When education for their children became accessible, these family clans coalesced into communities around the new schools. The communities gave rise to more churches, which eventually reached a total of 60 congregations spread out along the rivers. In 1971, the Mennonite Brethren churches, which had formed under the Dirks' ministry on the Tambo, joined with the Ashaninka congregations started by Wycliffe Bible Translators on the upper Ene and, along with small groups of Seventh Day Adventist believers in between, formed the Ashaninka Evangelical Church. In effect, the tribe created its own ecclesiastical system. This was on the advice of the missionaries, who taught the Ashaninka to promote fellowship and minimize competition within the body of Christ.

In 1969, Paul and Maurine Friesen moved from Atalaya to the campus of the Swiss Indian Mission, near Pucallpa, to teach in the inter-tribal Bible institute there. Despite the distance, the Friesens continued to work closely with the Ashaninka of the Ucayali, Tambo and Ene Rivers. Over the next 30 years, in fact, many students from that area came to study at the Swiss Indian Mission. The Ashaninka Evangelical Church eventually asked Paul to serve as an adviser to the organization.

Education between missionaries and natives was always a two-way affair. For their part, the Ashaninka taught the missionaries valuable skills, like hunting, fishing and growing manioc, yams and bananas. The missionaries and the natives played together, as well, football and volleyball mainly. When Paul Friesen plays volleyball, which he still does regularly at the age of 70, the rugged Kansan towers over the compact, brown-skinned Ashaninka. When he talks about the impact the Christian gospel has had on their way of life, the piercing blue eyes fairly blaze.

The real infrastructure and the unifying element of the tribe are the bilingual school system and the evangelical church. It's been in their own language, 100 per cent under their own leadership, they have the say-so. Over half the tribe is literate. They can read and write in their own language as well as Spanish. The Ashaninka church and the school system have unified the people. That's where they got the strength to defend themselves against Shining Path.

There were probably several reasons why they didn't go along with the Path. For one, the *senderistas* were outsiders, so they didn't want to work with them. Secondly, having title to their land gave the Ashaninka a sense of identity. They didn't want to lose it. They did not want anybody from the outside coming in and controlling them.

Also, the Ashaninka realized that the *senderistas* were doing things that, as Christians, they could not do. The gospel, in a general sense, gave the people a moral and spiritual base to resist. In a specific sense, it gave courage to leaders to say 'We will not join you because we are Christians.' They didn't give the Path any cooperation. When the *senderistas* realized that they couldn't win the people over peacefully, they began to use force.

*   *   *

Rafael Santoma received shocking news when he returned home to Camajeni after a three-day trip up the Tambo River to visit Ashaninka evangelical churches. During his absence, 60 Shining Path guerrillas had entered Camajeni and demanded that its residents pledge support to the revolution. Three men, Oscar Chimanga, Dante Martinez, a member of the neighbouring Yanesha tribe, and Santoma's 25-year-old brother Pablo, pointedly refused to do so. The *senderistas* hacked the three men to death with machetes while their families and neighbours watched helplessly. Before they left, the terrorists threatened the rest of the villagers with similar punishment unless they submitted.'And you had better be careful not to tell the army about this,' they said.

It was 1989 and Shining Path was on the move. In accordance with the Grand Plan of Deployment in the War of All Wars issued by Presidente Gonzalo, cadres were making their way down the Apurimac valley from Ayacucho and into the central jungle. Their objective: to liberate the communities along the Ene, Tambo and Ucayali Rivers and establish jungle bases there. Liberated communities would supply food for Shining Path guerrillas deployed in the highlands, as well as for those deployed in the central jungle. Once the Path had established a strong presence in the central jungle, its troops would continue up the Ucayali to the Amazon. By then, half the country would be in the hands of the Path and the other half would be at its mercy. Only one thing stood between the *senderistas* and the completion of this objective: the Ashaninka.

What happened in Camajeni happened in scores of communities along the rivers that run through the central jungle. In the week following the murder of the three men who had publicly rejected the Path, community leaders in Camajeni discussed what they should do. They realized that joining the *senderistas* would mean virtual slavery. The terrorists would force the villagers to turn over their crops of beans, rice, manioc and bananas to the revolution, leaving them little food to feed their families. In fact, Camajeni families already faced a food shortage because the terrorists had slaughtered part of their cattle and confiscated the remainder. They knew that if they refused to join the revolution, more community leaders would die. The terrorists would burn the village to the ground and intern the rest of them in concentration camps. It had already happened to scores of Ashaninka communities along the rivers. Camajeni had no option but to disappear.

Before the *senderistas* knew anything about it, the 25 families of Camajeni had packed up all the tools, pots, pans, food and clothing they could carry and slipped away one night down the Tambo to Betania, a town near Atalaya where a Navy base protected them from Shining Path 'liberation'. Betania, like other secured communities in the central jungle, was turning into a refugee camp. Over eight hundred Ashaninkas had taken up residence there. Once they arrived, the refugees unpacked their household possessions and began clearing patches of jungle to plant manioc, yams and bananas. Farm land around the town soon became scarce, due to growing population pressure. The Camajeni refugees desperately needed to grow food for themselves, however, for they would not return to their home upriver for six long years.

*   *   *

The village of Potsoteni lay near the banks of the Ene, a three-day boat trip upriver from Atalaya. In February 1989, the Path paid a visit to Potsoteni. Unlike the Ashaninka of Camajeni, Potsoteni villagers knew the *senderistas* were coming. The local school teacher and his wife had invited Shining Path to the village. The couple were *atsiri*, outsiders brought by the government to teach the children of Potsoteni, not bilingual teachers. The teacher and his wife, the Ashaninkas learned, had developed admiration for the Path while studying in university. They told the villagers that it was in their best interest to come to the people's meeting and hear what the *senderistas* had to say.

Pedro Aurelio was about to leave Potsoteni for Pucallpa to study the Bible at the Swiss Indian Mission when the Path came to expound the Marxist-Leninist-Maoist doctrine of Presidente Gonzalo. Aurelio instinctively knew the political theory he heard that day went against the teachings of the Word of God.

> The terrorists held a meeting to make us understand what their purpose was. While talking about that, they explained how they wanted to bring together Ashaninka from the whole Ene River region. They wanted to organize a struggle against the rich, against the military. Their purpose was to destroy.
>
> For us evangelical Christians, what they wanted to do was not right. We had become acquainted with the Word of God and it says we should not be anxious or covet the riches of this world. We have an obligation to defend ourselves with the Word. We could not accept their politics. We totally rejected it. They left. A few days later they returned, threatening to kill us because we did not accept them.

Pedro Aurelio himself was absent when the *senderistas* returned. A letter had arrived in the interim from Paul Friesen, notifying Pedro that a bush plane would arrive at the airstrip in Atalaya within days to carry him and his family to the Bible Institute in Pucallpa to enrol. The Aurelios packed what few belongings they could carry, took leave of their relatives and neighbours in Potsoteni and headed downriver to Atalaya. What happened next, Pedro learned through letters his family sent to him at the Swiss Indian Mission.

The Path appeared the second time in Potsoteni two weeks after the first visit. 'Join us, and we'll see that you have everything you'll ever need,' they promised. The community declined the offer, despite the insistence of the school teacher and his wife that it was in their best interests. The *senderistas* finally lost patience with the stubborn Ashaninka. Suddenly pointing their guns at Oscar Andrés, pastor of the Ashaninka Evangelical Church in Potsoteni, they said: 'All right, you're coming with us. We must re-educate you.' The terrorists led

Pastor Andrés out of the village at gunpoint. The following evening, they returned for Sandoval Eusebio, president of the community council. 'We are taking your leader to our base to talk,' they told the villagers. 'Once he understands the purpose of our revolution, we are sure he will want you all to join us.'

The *senderistas* did not talk much with either President Eusebio or Pastor Andrés. Instead, they conducted the two men several kilometres upriver, lashed them to wooden poles, smashed their skulls with heavy rocks and threw their bodies into the river. Several days later, an Ashaninka from a neighbouring village found the bodies there and informed the men of Potsoteni.

The terrorists expected the killings to produce two results. One, eliminate troublesome leaders and two, coerce the headstrong Ashaninka to submit to the revolution. It appeared they had achieved their objectives. When the school teacher in Potsoteni announced that the *senderistas* would return a third time to liberate the community once and for all, the villagers did not protest. They even agreed to throw a party to celebrate liberation. They even agreed to make *masato* to serve at the celebration.

No important Ashaninka celebration is complete without potent *masato*. The natives make it by adding water to boiled manioc and yams, pulverizing the mixture and allowing it to ferment for several days. 'We will make the *masato* good and strong for the *senderistas*,' Alejandro Aurelio, Pedro's brother, assured the school teacher. His compliant attitude pleased the teacher. Evidently, the headstrong Ashaninka had finally realized that it was in their best interests to submit to the revolution.

This was not precisely the case. For while some of the villagers made *masato*, Alejandro Aurelio directed others to make *balsas*. The *balsa*, named after the buoyant wood of which it is made, is the preferred Ashaninka mode of river transport. Poles 30 centimetres or so in diameter are cut into 2-metre lengths and lashed together with palm fibres. Skilled *balsa* builders can put one together in two hours. The Ashaninka use a *balsa* to float downriver to their destination, then discard it. The current in the rivers of the central jungle is too swift to use a *balsa* for upriver transport. The Ashaninka purchase passage for those trips on one of the motorized long boats that ply the waterways. Motorized transport costs the Ashaninka many times as much as a *balsa*, hence he prefers to use the homemade raft whenever possible. He also prefers to use the *balsa* when stealth is necessary.

In this case, the villagers of Potsoteni used considerable stealth to build their *balsas*. They chose a site one hour's walk from the village to cut the poles and lash them together with palm fibres. They hid the finished rafts in the brush along the river's edge. During the few days they awaited the return of the *senderistas*, villagers furtively transferred tools, pots, pans, food and clothing from their huts to the brush by the river's edge. All was ready when the celebration began.

The entire village turned out to welcome the Path that evening. Goodwill seemed to flow as freely as the *masato*. At Alejandro Aurelio's urging, the Ashaninka continually refilled their guests' drinking vessels. As the party wore on, the merriment intensified. By midnight, in fact, the *senderistas* and the school teachers were enjoying the celebration so much they did not notice half the village slipping away into the night. Ten families, including the entire membership of the Ashaninka Evangelical Church of Potsoteni, stole to the river's edge, loaded their household belongings onto *balsas* and launched them into the swift current.

Their escape cost them dearly. In the darkness, Huber Maravi poled his *balsa* into a treacherous whirlpool. It sucked the craft under water, dumping Huber, his wife Edia and their two small children into the swift current. Huber resurfaced to see another boatman pulling Edia to safety. He searched frantically for his two-year-old son and one-year-old daughter, but could find no trace of them in the blackness. The river had taken the little ones.

Under Alejandro Aurelio's guidance, the remaining *balsas* negotiated the journey downriver without further mishap. Two days later, the ten refugee families arrived at their destination, the town of Poyeni. There they unpacked their household

possessions and discarded the *balsas*. Unlike their other jour-
neys, they did not purchase passage upriver on a motorized
long boat, for they would not return to their homes for five
long years.

When, on the morning after their escape, the *senderistas*
back in Potsoteni had roused themselves from the *masato*-
induced stupor to discover that only the school teacher, his
wife and 30 or so of the Ashaninka remained under their liberation, they were understandably upset. They told the villagers that they would be moving away from Potsoteni soon, in
order to grow rice and beans for the revolution. None of the
Ashaninka they took away with them were believing
Christians, so the terrorists heard no more protest. These
Ashaninka would serve the revolution, as ordered. In fact,
some of them would die for the revolution, as ordered.

*   *   *

'By and large, the Ashaninka people have been pacifist,' Paul
Friesen says. 'They retire from conflict rather than go out
deliberately to engage in it. They've had to defend themselves,
but haven't really gone out for vengeance. That's a good sign.
However, sooner or later that will break if the terrorists keep
on. Then there will be a hotter war between the people.'

By the end of 1989, the Ashaninka living on the Pinchis
River decided they could no longer retire from the conflict.
On the evening of 8 December, armed guerrillas of the Tupac
Amaru Revolutionary Movement, known by its Spanish
acronym MRTA, arrived at the Puerto Bermudez home of
Alejandro Calderón, the Great Chief of the Ashaninka. The
guerrillas asked Calderón to come with them to an important
meeting. They assured the Great Chief that his attendance at
the meeting was of vital importance to the interests of his
people. They mentioned that two other members of the tribal
council, Rodrigo Chauca and Benjamin Cavero, would be at
the meeting, as well. With this news, Calderón agreed to
accompany the guerrillas. He was never seen alive again.

The MRTA guerrillas, allies of Shining Path, held Calderón
for several days before executing him. They justified their

crime on the absurd charge that Calderón had helped capture Máximo Velando during the ill-fated Revolutionary Left uprising of 1965. They actually intended to keep Calderón's murder a secret for a time, but Benjamin Cavero escaped from his abductors, made his way back to Puerto Bermudez and informed his fellow Ashaninka of the crime. When tribal leaders learned of the Great Chief's death, they decided it was time to defend themselves. On Christmas Day, warriors from 56 communities in the Pinchis River district gathered in council in Puerto Bermudez and declared war on MRTA and their Shining Path allies.

News of the Calderón murder spread rapidly through the central jungle, as did word of the Ashaninka army mustering to avenge the death of the Great Chief. In January, the Yanesha of the Grand Pajonal region arrived in Puerto Bermudez to pledge their solidarity with the Ashaninka in the campaign against MRTA and the Path. The war councils of the two tribes agreed to seal off the Pinchis River district and the Grand Pajonal region to outsiders. The tribes could do this because the Ashaninka and Yanesha control these areas completely. Unlike the land on the upper Ucayali, Tambo and Ene Rivers, which Ashaninka communities share with migrant highlanders, the Pinchis and the Grand Pajonal lay under full tribal sovereignty. No *atsiri* lived there. Native councils agreed to issue identification documents to the few outsiders whose assigned duties took them into tribal lands – government officials, missionaries, teachers and such. Everybody else trespassing on tribal lands would be arrested and, if they could not establish a justifiable reason for being there, executed. Tribal leaders announced these terms in the public media, of course. News of the ban spread rapidly through the central jungles and, as expected, most outsiders stayed away from tribal lands. For those few who defied the ban, warriors dug pit traps on jungle trails and filled them with sharpened bamboo stakes and poisonous snakes. Any outsider who fell into a pit trap would not defy the ban a second time.

Of course, the only outsiders who defied the ban were the terrorists who had come to make war on the Ashaninka and Yanesha. Tribal leaders calculated that, once everybody else had abandoned the Pinchis River and Grand Pajonal, the terrorists would be easy to spot. By April, in fact, the Ashaninka army had spotted a large guerrilla base hidden on tribal lands. Warriors armed with shotguns, blow guns, bows and arrows silently massed for battle. All was ready when a driving rainstorm struck. Because of the bad weather, the guerrillas relaxed their guard, believing military action to be impossible under such conditions. The Ashaninka believed bad weather to be as good as any for military action and attacked. When the slaughter ended, the entire contingent of 160 terrorists lay dead in the jungle. The Ashaninka suffered no casualties.

For four months, the Ashaninka army and their Yanesha allies combed the jungle for clandestine cadres of MRTA and Shining Path guerrillas. When found, the terrorists died without pity at the hands of the natives. By the end of July, some 250 guerrillas who had tried to incite revolution on tribal lands of the Pinchis River and the Grand Pajonal had died there. The rest fled, leaving the Ashaninka and Yanesha in peace.

Peace was all the Ashaninka really cared about. 'If you had not killed our Great Chief, we would not have made war on you,' tribal leaders announced to the Path through the public media. The natives had avenged the murder of Alejandro Calderón and sought no further vengeance against the terrorists. At the end of July, the campaign ended and most of the army went home, for the Ashaninka, despite their well-deserved reputation as adept warriors, prefer to live in peace with everybody else.

5

Dangerous Business

In 1979, within a week of his graduation from Bible college in California, Rómulo Sauñe arrived in Peru with his new wife, Donna Jackson, a blonde, blue-eyed American. Despite her US origins, Donna was as much at home in Peru as her husband. Her parents, missionaries with Wycliffe Bible Translators, had brought Donna to Peru as an infant and brought her up at the mission's jungle base near Pucallpa. Rómulo met her there while working on Quechua scripture translation with Conrad Phelps and his wife, Irma, a native of Cuzco.

Donna and Rómulo shared a passion that sparked their romance and bonded them in marriage. It was a passion for translating the Bible into the languages of Andean peoples and teaching them to read it. Thousands of missionaries around the world shared the same passion, giving up lucrative careers and comfortable lifestyles to spend their time translating the Bible. In the Sauñes' case, their passion would lead to great sacrifice. Upon their arrival in Ayacucho, the couple found that Bible translation had become dangerous. Life-threatening, in fact. Several of Rómulo's former schoolmates and teachers were now active in Shining Path. They knew of his passion for Bible translation and did not approve.

'These missionaries you work with are Yankee imperialists and their Bible is nothing more than imperialist propaganda,' they warned Rómulo. 'If you continue with this translation business, we will consider you a traitor to the revolution.'

Rómulo and Donna did continue. Late one night, 16 terrorists armed with machine guns surrounded their house, cut the electric wires and broke down the door, intent on shooting the Sauñes in their sleep. But Rómulo and Donna were not at home.

They had visited a Quechua church that day and stayed overnight in the country. Only Rómulo's teenage brother Ruben was in the house and he managed to scramble into the attic to escape the *senderistas*.

Rómulo decided to move Donna and their infant son, Romi, to the relative safety of Lima. Danger followed him to the capital. One evening, there came an unexpected knock at the door. On his way to answer it, Rómulo experienced a strong, inner urge not to do so. He stood listening to the loud knocking, but did not open the door. The callers eventually left. Next morning, one of them returned.

'If you had opened your door last night, you would be dead this morning,' the *senderista* told Rómulo. 'God must have warned you.' The guerrilla explained that his job was to infiltrate evangelical churches and learn their beliefs, in order to train other young terrorists how to subvert Christians to Shining Path. 'I've memorized a lot of Bible verses for this assignment,' he said. 'All night those texts have been pounding in my head. I can't stand it any longer.'

The young man knelt beside Rómulo and, with loud weeping, asked God for forgiveness. 'As a sign of my repentance, I'm giving you this,' he said, handing Rómulo a list of churches, Bible institutes and seminaries in Lima. 'Shining Path has planned a coordinated bombing of these places. I want you to alert the authorities. And please, help me escape. I can't go back to the Path ever again.'

Rómulo took the young man out of town in his car, dropped Donna and Romi at the Wycliffe translation centre where they would be safe, and took the list of bombing targets to police headquarters. At first, the officers did not believe his story. When they learned he was a native of Ayacucho, they accused him of being a *senderista* himself and submitted Rómulo to questioning. Fortunately, a senior officer learned of the incident and intervened before things got ugly. 'This man is telling the truth,' he told his subordinates. 'We have just captured a terrorist with documented plans to bomb the Christian and Missionary Alliance church next Sunday.'

Peruvian authorities deployed security forces at the churches and Bible seminaries on the list Rómulo provided them. No bombings occurred. Nevertheless, the near tragedy indicated that Christianity itself had become dangerous business in Peru.

*   *   *

Ayacucho, November 1982

Higher education in Peru was becoming dangerous as well. Lea Yupanqui, the 20-year-old granddaughter of Justiniano and Teofila Quicaña, was studying biology at the National University of San Cristobal of Huamanga when the Path liberated the school. Liberation meant that revolutionary slogans appeared on walls all over the campus and no one – not students, faculty or staff – dared remove them. Liberation meant that if the Path declared a general strike, everyone – students, faculty and staff – abandoned their classrooms and offices to attend people's meetings or, if ordered to do so, marched in protest demonstrations through the streets of Ayacucho. Liberation meant that no one on the campus of the University of San Cristobal could speak or write ideas opposed to the Path and its revolution. Those who did suffered swift revolutionary justice.

Lea witnessed revolutionary justice in her classroom. In some incidents, hooded *senderistas* burst into the room in the midst of the lecture. Announcing that a certain student had broken Shining Path laws, they hastily executed the offender in front of the class, then disappeared out the door. No one dared touch the dead body. Informants took note of anyone who showed sympathy for an enemy of the revolution and reported it to the Path. That person could become the next victim of revolutionary justice. So, until the police came to remove the corpse, classmates and professor tried to appear disinterested in the murder victim.

Lea Yupanqui endured three semesters of Shining Path terror at the National University of San Cristobal of Huamanga. Like the vast majority of the students there, she did not endorse the Path's revolutionary agenda. She simply wanted to get an education and this university was the only option she had. The daughter of Rufina Quicaña, a flower merchant, and Rafael Yupanqui, a Presbyterian pastor, Lea could not afford to go elsewhere to study. Like most of the students, faculty and staff at the University of San Cristobal, Lea suffered in silence, hoping desperately to graduate before falling victim to the terror.

The terror intensified when the military occupied Ayacucho and began carrying out orders to eradicate the Path from the National University of San Cristobal of Huamanga. To do so, the army arrested hundreds of students, faculty and staff – typically in clandestine, night-time raids – whom they suspected of being *senderistas*. The vast majority of those arrested, whether *senderistas* or not, were never again seen alive.

One night while the Yupanqui family slept, hooded soldiers broke down the door of their home. Yelling and cursing, they forced the Yupanquis to lie on the parlour floor while they searched the house.

'What are you looking for?' Rufina asked.

'Guns,' they replied. 'Do you have guns?'

'No, we have no guns, only these flowers.' Rufina showed the soldiers the dozens of bouquets she and her daughters had prepared for sale on All Saints Day.

The soldiers cursed. 'Which one is she?' they asked a companion. Rufina noticed a small, hooded figure that was not dressed in military uniform. Whether it was man, woman or child, she could not tell. The figure pointed at Lea. 'It's her, it's her!' it screamed. The soldiers pulled Lea to her feet, tied her hands, threw a red hood over her head and dragged her from the house. Rufina and Rafael stared at one another, then broke into tears. Rufina ran from the house to beg the soldiers not to take her daughter, but they were gone. Rufina fell to the ground, unconscious.

The Yupanquis spent the remainder of the night praying and weeping. Next day, Rafael and Rufina began to look for their missing daughter. They started with the police, searching from precinct to precinct. No, Lea Yupanqui had not been detained by officers of this unit, they all said. Next they tried the hospitals and morgues. There they encountered other mothers and fathers weeping inconsolably for sons and daughters, but did not find Lea. Then, although they hoped their search would likewise be in vain, they searched the ravines and gullies on the outskirts of town.

These were the places where both the army and Shining Path disposed of the bodies of their victims. The most-used dumping grounds were *Puracuti* and *Infiernillo*, 'Little Hell'. Mr and Mrs Yupanqui searched through the corpses littering these ravines. Dogs had chewed some of the bodies, others had decomposed, making identification difficult. Mr and Mrs Yupanqui knew that, if necessary, they could identify Lea by her clothing. To their relief, they did not find her in the ravines.

For two weeks they searched. They went to the army base. The soldiers could not, or would not, tell them if Lea was in their custody. Rufina begged them. 'Please, for the love of your own mothers, if you have my daughter here, give her a cup of water, something to eat. Please, see that she has a blanket. Don't let her die of the cold.'

Lea did not risk dying either of hunger or cold. Shining Path suspects did not live long enough for that. The night she was abducted, she sat in the back of an army truck among a dozen other hooded prisoners. Soldiers screamed curses at them. 'You are no-good terrorists! We are going to kill you all!' Although Lea could see only the ground at her feet, she knew the truck was climbing the highway out of Ayacucho. She commended her soul to God, thinking the soldiers would kill her as soon as they reached the edge of town and throw her body into a ravine. After more than an hour, the truck arrived at the Pisco Tambo military base. The suspects were taken from the truck and thrown together into bare concrete cells. They would remain there, bound and hooded, 24 hours a day, for their entire captivity. Even though it was the middle of the night, Lea was unable to sleep.

Each night, soldiers selected prisoners from the cells for interrogation. They took them to another bare room, stripped them of their clothing and hung them from the ceiling by their wrists, arms behind the back. A few suspects passed out from the agonizing pain, others passed out from their interrogators' brutal kicks and blows. Some succumbed to the beatings and gave the interrogators what they wanted: the names of more Shining Path suspects, whom they would arrest and submit to the same torment. If suspects did not give the information, the interrogators applied electric shock to their private parts or plunged them in tanks of icy water until they either passed out or gave them names.

Lea would never learn the identity of the small, hooded person who accused her of being a *senderista*. It may have been a classmate who had broken under the torture and, vainly believing that the interrogators would fulfil their promise of release in return for names, accused Lea. It may have been a street urchin who happened to know Lea's name and address and, for a bit of reward money or a meal, led the soldiers to her house. Lea was not, of course, a *senderista*. But that did not matter. She was not the first innocent student in Peru seized and tortured by the security forces; nor would she be the last.

Torture, not hunger or cold, killed many Shining Path suspects. One night, soldiers returned an unconscious prisoner, bound and hooded, to the cell where Lea was being kept. The man never regained consciousness. The next night, soldiers removed his corpse from the cell and disposed of it, most likely by casting it into *Infiernillo*. Cellmates told Lea the man had been their professor at the National University of San Cristobal of Huamanga.

In the course of their searching for Lea, Rafael and Rufina Yupanqui learned about these nightly torture sessions. From then on, they gathered their remaining children in the family parlour every evening to pray for Lea's safety. 'Holy Spirit, preserve my daughter's life,' Rufina prayed. 'Please, spare her from terrible pain, see that she gets something to eat and a blanket.'

After two weeks of praying and searching, Rafael and Rufina decided that Lea was in God's hands and they could do no more. One morning three weeks after Lea's abduction, Rufina awoke in a strangely cheerful mood. 'Lea is coming home today,' she told Rafael, 'I saw it in my dream. Soldiers brought her to our door, wrapped in a blanket. Lea cried to me, "Mama, I'm home!" I ran to the officer and asked him, "What is the

name of your commander? I want to thank him."" Don't ask,"
he said. "It's enough you have your daughter back."'

'I think she will come back, too,' Rafael told his wife.
Although he had not dreamed it, he felt God telling him it
would be so.

Later that day, Manuel Segura, a fellow pastor, came to console the Yupanqui family, something he had often done since
Lea's disappearance. 'Don't worry, brother,' Rufina and Rafael
told him, 'our daughter is coming home tonight.' All day as
she worked in her vegetable plot, Rufina hummed gospel
tunes and smiled to herself, knowing Lea was coming home.

At 9.00 p.m., soldiers took Lea from her cell. She trembled
as they led her down the hallway, assuming she was on her
way to an interrogation session. Instead they loaded her onto
the back of an army truck. 'Now it is my turn to die,' she
thought to herself. She knew she was the only one left alive of
those who had been arrested with her. She had given her
interrogators none of the information they wanted, so they
had run out of patience. Once again she commended her soul
to God.

Later that night, someone knocked on the Yupanquis' front
door. Rafael ran to answer it.

'Don't go to the door! We don't know who it is,' Rufina cautioned. 'It might be the soldiers again.'

'It's my daughter, I know it is!' Rafael said. He opened the
door and there on the steps, thin and pale but alive, stood Lea.

When she was able to talk, Lea told her parents about her
ordeal, about the terror, the torture and the killings. 'But for
some reason, the soldiers gave me a mattress to sleep on and
clean water – not the briny stuff they usually gave prisoners.
"We don't know why we are treating you so well," they would
say. But they kept doing it.

'And there's something else,' she added. 'The soldiers inter-
rogated me very little, not every night like my cellmates. I
would not have survived otherwise. I don't know why they
treated me that way.'

Rufina knew. It was because the Holy Spirit had answered
her prayers.

*   *   *

Between them, Shining Path and the Peruvian army gradually converted Chakiqpampa into a ghost town. As with most Quechua communities in rural Huamanga, its residents fled to Ayacucho to avoid Shining Path atrocities or else moved into 'security camps' that the military had established around Vinchos and other towns. The few who stayed to work their fields and graze their livestock took to sleeping in caves in the mountain slopes above the village in order to avoid contact with either Shining Path or the army.

Zoila Quicaña Sauñe was forced to abandon the country home she and Enrique had maintained in Chakiqpampa since their move to Ayacucho 20 years before. On one of her visits to the village, Shining Path informed her they wanted the house, which sat on the edge of a level field, for their head-quarters. 'From here, we can shoot at army helicopters when they land.' Zoila did not answer. But when the *senderistas* had gone, she hired seven horses from a neighbour, packed all the chickens, potatoes, grain, tools, pots, pans and dishes she had at the house on the animals and headed to Ayacucho.

Before leaving, she pleaded with her aged parents to come away with her. 'What for?' Justiniano and Teofila asked. 'The *senderistas* don't bother old people like us. We will be all right.'

Zoila knew Shining Path would try to punish her and Enrique for 'deserting the revolution'. The Path depended on peasant families like the Sauñes for food, which they often exacted from them at gunpoint. Sure enough, some weeks after Zoila abandoned her Chakiqpampa house, terrorists located the Sauñes at the Quicapata Wycliffe centre where they were working as caretakers. The Path's night-time attack on the centre failed, however. The Quicapata guard dogs set up such a howl that the terrorists fled. Later Zoila and Enrique learned the police had killed the guerrilla band. They suffered no more attacks.

Back in Chakiqpampa, Justiniano and Teofila Quicaña maintained a precarious relationship with the *senderistas* who came by from time to time asking for food. The elderly couple fed them such as they had, partly out of fear, partly in com-pliance with the Andean code of hospitality, and partly so that Justiniano could preach the gospel to them. The veteran evangelist even passed out New Testaments to the young guerrillas, some of whom actually read the Yankee imperialist propaganda.

From time to time, the guerrillas made clumsy attempts at fostering goodwill among the few remaining residents of Chakiqpampa. Once when the Quicañas' daughter Antonia was visiting, the Path arrived with supplies of clothing, soft drinks and fruit cake to share with the Quechua peasants. Antonia, who owned a small dry-goods shop in Ayacucho, refused to accept any of the gifts, aware they had come from lorries the *senderistas* had hijacked on the road from Lima. To her, the merchandise embodied the tears of modest shop-keepers, like herself, who had lost hard-earned money in the robbery.

'Please, sell the few animals you have left and come live with us in the city,' Antonia urged her aged parents when she was ready to return to Ayacucho.

'What in the world for?' Teofila replied. 'My life is here. Besides, the *senderistas* don't bother old people like us.'

One day not long after that, an army unit arrived at the Quicaña home with several Quechua peasants in tow. Justiniano was not home so Teofila went to meet them. 'These are the people who brought the *senderistas* here,' her neighbours told the soldiers, pointing at Teofila. 'They tried to force us to join the Path.'

'That's not true!' Teofila protested.

'Do you give food to the terrorists?' asked the officer in charge.

'Sir, we are Christians. We give food to anyone who asks for it.' Teofila looked closely at the group of Quechuas and realized not one of them was a Christian. She also noticed they were all Chankas.

'You will come with us,' the officer said. Some of his soldiers began to round up the Quicañas' animals while others rummaged through their home and removed everything of value. When they finished, they set fire to the house.

Justiniano Quicaña watched all this from a distant mountain

slope. When he saw the soldiers take Teofila away, he began walking to Ayacucho as fast as his aged legs could carry him.

The soldiers took Teofila to their base in Chupacc, determined to get information out of her about the Path. To do this, they stripped off her clothing, tied her hands and feet and plunged her in a tank of icy water, three times. Each time she came up, she insisted she knew nothing about the Path. After her third plunge into the water and trembling from cold and exhaustion, Teofila fainted. The soldiers let her lie where she fell, thinking she would die. 'Nobody cares about that old woman anyway,' they smirked. Teofila's neighbours watched the torture but did nothing to help. Some awaited interrogation themselves and dared not arouse suspicion by showing sympathy to a suspected terrorist.

As she awakened from unconsciousness, Teofila saw the white dove. She knew it to be a dove, even though none like it lived in rural Huamanga. The bird hovered over her as Teofila opened her eyes. The old woman smiled. She no longer shivered from cold and fear. Teofila mouthed a quiet prayer. 'Lord, you have not abandoned me. You truly are at my side. Thank you, Lord.'

When the officer in charge returned, he was surprised to see Teofila dressed and sitting quietly on the grass. 'Take this one to the kitchen and put her to work,' he ordered. 'We will deal with her later.'

Several of Teofila's neighbours were already at work in the kitchen. They were surprised, and of course delighted, they said, to see her alive. Later Teofila overheard one woman whisper to another: 'They say tomorrow the soldiers are going to put our old auntie before the firing squad in the town plaza.' The comment did not upset Teofila. Her vision of the hovering dove had granted her an extraordinary sense of peace.

The soldiers did not put Teofila before the firing squad. Next day, a neatly dressed businesswoman from Ayacucho appeared and asked to talk with the officer in charge. 'My name is Antonia Quicaña and I want you to release my mother Teofila,' she said.

Justiniano Quicaña had reached the city the day after Teofila's arrest and told his children what happened. Despite their fears that Teofila might already be dead, Antonia and her younger sister Rebeca immediately left for Chakiqpampa to intercede for their mother. None of the villagers would take them into their homes, so the sisters spent the night in a cave. Next day, Antonia walked on alone to Chupacc. On the way, she met acquaintances coming from the town. 'Don't go there! They will kill you, too,' they warned. 'I have never had any dealings with the Path,' Antonia countered. 'My conscience is clear.'

Antonia's poise impressed the officer in charge. When he saw that someone did care about 'that old woman' and that the someone was not going anywhere without her, he ordered Teofila released. Antonia walked back to Chakiqpampa with her mother, herding a cow, eight sheep and 20 goats, all that was left of the Quicañas' livestock. The soldiers had slaughtered and roasted the rest. The women could not remain in Chakiqpampa, of course, since the house was in ashes, so Antonia finally convinced her aged mother to come and live in the relative safety of Ayacucho.

Teofila and Justiniano put up with city life for nearly four months. Then planting season came round and they could endure it no longer. Their children reluctantly returned the aged couple to Chakiqpampa to rebuild their *adobe* home, recover their few remaining animals and plant their fields of potatoes and grain.

*   *   *

3 September 1987 was one of the most tearful days in Rómulo Sauñe's life.

Rómulo had come to Ayacucho from Chosica, the quiet community near Lima where he and Donna now lived. There the Sauñes had established Runa Simi, a literacy training centre for native Andean peoples. 'Runa simi' is the Quechua term for their language; it literally means 'the word of man'. The focus of activity at the Runa Simi centre in Chosica, however, was the Word of God. There the Sauñes worked with Wycliffe missionaries Homer Emerson, Conrad and Irma Phelps and others to translate the Old Testament into the Ayacucho dialect of Quechua. It had taken 11 years to accomplish, but now all

66 books of scripture existed in the language of Huamanga. On this September day, the United Bible Society would dedicate the *Ayacucho Bible* in a public ceremony in the city and release it for sale to the public.

The sale of the Bibles concerned Rómulo, especially when he arrived in Ayacucho to find hundreds of colourfully dressed Quechuas awaiting the dedication ceremony. The Bible Society had shipped 4,000 copies of the *Ayacucho Bible* for the dedication, but Rómulo knew that would not be nearly enough.

'We don't expect to sell more than a few hundred copies to start with,' officials told Rómulo when he urged them to send more. 'Most of the Quechuas can't read. Why would they pay three dollars, which is a lot of money to them, for a book they can't read?'

'They will buy it because it is their book,' Rómulo insisted. 'After all, they helped translate it.'

Rómulo's translation team had tried an innovative approach to Bible translation. To check the accuracy of the first drafts, they read entire Old Testament books aloud to hundreds of listeners at Quechua church conferences, then asked for suggestions to clarify meaning and improve readability. 'Thank you for your help,' Rómulo would tell the crowds upon concluding the readings. 'And remember, this translation of the Scriptures is as much your work as it is ours.'

The personal involvement of Quechua believers in the translation process aroused great interest in the *Ayacucho Bible* throughout rural Huamanga. So great, in fact, that once Bible Society officials offered the dedicatory prayer and opened the boxes of new scriptures, a mass of colourfully dressed Quechuas surged forward to purchase them. In less than an hour, the 4,000 copies had disappeared. Then the tears began to flow.

Grown Quechua men wept because they could not buy Bibles. Some had walked to Ayacucho from villages two or three days distant. They carried extra money, collected from neighbours who could not make the journey themselves, planning to carry Bibles back to them. Now they must go home empty-handed. Some of them followed Rómulo Sauñe away from the dedication ceremony, weeping and pleading as they went. Rómulo could do nothing but weep, as well. But his were tears of joy. He knew now, beyond a doubt, that 11 years of sacrifice, toil and danger had been worth it.

*   *   *

Chakiqpampa, 11 December 1989

All the men were gone from Chakiqpampa. The day before, a messenger came to tell them that the Path was coming from Huancavelica, bent on revolutionary justice. No one knew which of the village leaders had offended the guerrillas, nor which offences the *senderistas* intended to punish, so all the men left town together. Except for Justiniano Quicaña. Nearly deaf despite the hearing aid a missionary friend had given him, Justiniano did not hear the warning to evacuate. By the time he realized the rest of the men had gone, it was already late. 'Just as well,' he told Teofila, 'I'm too old to run. Besides, the *senderistas* won't bother an old man like me.'

Just after dawn on that December morning, five terrorists passed the Quicaña home on their way into the village. Justiniano watched them pass. 'Go down there and see what they're saying,' he told Teofila. By the time she arrived in the village, the *senderistas* had gathered the women and children in the plaza. Their failure to find any men in town irritated the terrorists. 'Start marching,' they ordered the women and children. 'We're taking you to Culluhuanca.'

Culluhuanca was a Chanka community on the slopes above Chakiqpampa. As they turned toward it, Teofila looked up the hill toward her house to see a band of *senderistas* descending from the direction of Culluhuanca. They carried bundles of dry grass. When they reached the Quicaña home, the terrorists began to pile the bundles around the walls. Teofila knew in an instant they intended to burn down her house. She hurried home.

'So, you are the old man who preaches the gospel,' the *senderistas* were saying to Justiniano. 'They told us in Culluhuanca that you are the reason why there are so many

Christians around here. Always talking about God, confusing the people. They said we ought to kill you.'

'Look at this thing in his ear,' one terrorist said, pointing to the hearing aid. 'I think he uses it to communicate with Yankee imperialists.'

'For sure, you use this tongue of yours to dupe the people,' the first terrorist said to Justiniano, wagging a finger in his face. 'We're going to have to cut it out.'

When Teofila arrived, she saw that the *senderistas* had looted her home and bundled everything of value in her best bedspread to carry away with them. They set fire to the building and flames engulfed the couple's furnishings and clothing. The terrorists pulled bayonets from their belts and prodded Justiniano and Teofila in the back. 'We're going to Culluhuanca,' they ordered. 'Start walking.'

Teofila knew it futile to protest. She started up the mountain slope. She had not gone far when she heard shouting below. She turned to see a terrorist strike Justiniano savagely on the head with the butt of his bayonet. Blood spurted from her husband's scalp.

'Get moving!' the *senderista* screamed at Justiniano.

'But can't you see I'm an old man?' Justiniano protested. 'I have to go slowly. I can't help it.'

Teofila recognized the terrorist badgering Justiniano. He was a Chanka who hated the Quicañas and Sauñes with a hatred passed down from his ancestors. That hatred was about to explode on her husband.

'Hurry, hurry!' Teofila shouted to Justiniano.

'I said to get moving!' the terrorist yelled, hitting Justiniano again with his bayonet butt. Justiniano fell to the ground. The *senderista* bent over and slashed the old man's throat with his bayonet.

'Stop!' Teofila screamed. 'Why are you killing my husband? What has he done?'

A terrorist prodded Teofila in the back with his bayonet. 'You want to die, too?' he mocked. 'You think we couldn't kill you the same way?' Several terrorists started toward Teofila. She turned abruptly and headed up the slope at a brisk walk. Her retreat rendered her unable to see what was happening to Justiniano, but it did save her life. The terrorists, unable to match her quick pace in the thin Andean air, did not overtake the petite woman.

When she reached Culluhuanca, the *senderistas* shut Teofila in a house with the rest of their captives while they discussed their next move. Presently, the beating blades of an approaching army helicopter interrupted their conversation. The terrorists hurriedly gathered their weapons and vanished.

Free of the terrorists, Teofila made her way back home. She found Justiniano's body lying where he fell. The two family dogs stood guard beside him. The bayonet had sliced so deeply that Justiniano's head was nearly severed from his body. The Chanka had carried out his threat to cut out the evangelist's tongue, mutilating his entire jaw in the process. The shock was so great, Teofila could not weep. She sat mutely beside Justiniano. After some time, she noticed the sun had climbed high overhead. Wearily, she pulled a piece of roofing tin from her ruined house to shield her husband's body from the heat.

The shock of Justiniano's brutal murder reverberated through the Quicaña–Sauñe clan. The news travelled quickly to Ayacucho, Chosica and beyond. The trauma struck Justiniano's grandson, Joshua Sauñe, particularly hard. Joshua had just arrived in Lima from Arizona following an eight-year absence. He brought with him his new bride, Missy, and was planning to take her to Chakiqpampa to introduce her to his grandfather. A sombre phone call from Ayacucho obliged Joshua to cancel his plans.

Tragic as was Justiniano Quicaña's death, it was also remarkable in that it had not happened sooner. He and his family espoused, very publicly, beliefs that Shining Path vowed to eradicate from Peruvian society. Yet, in the decade since the Path had launched its violent onslaught against Peruvian society, Justiniano was the first member of the Quicaña–Sauñe clan to die at the hands of terrorists.

Sadly, he would not be the last.

6

The Reunion

Several months after moving to Lima from Huánuco, Wycliffe missionaries Bruce and Jan Benson received a call from their friend Ruben Matías. Despite being blind, Matías pastored the Christian and Missionary Alliance church in the small town of San Jorge, near Tingo María. The Bensons were glad to hear from Matías. San Jorge was in a red zone controlled by Shining Path and Bruce and Jan worried about Matías and other evangelical pastors they knew there. Their concern for their friend's safety had increased considerably since the day the Path abducted and robbed them in Llata.

Ruben assured them that he was all right. 'Listen, there is a young man from my congregation in San Jorge I'd like you to meet,' he said. 'He just recently became a Christian. Could you join us for lunch at the Christian and Missionary Alliance church in Chorrillos?'

The Bensons said they could. At the Chorrillos luncheon, Matías introduced them to Jorge Rios. The man was 26 years old and had the physique of a middleweight boxer. For some reason, Jorge seemed ill at ease meeting the Bensons. 'How do you do, sir,' he said to Bruce cautiously. Bruce shook the young man's hand. Jorge tensed like a caged animal.

Bruce peered into the rugged face. 'Pardon me, but have we met?'

Jorge hesitated before answering. 'You don't know me, but I have seen you before. I was in the Shining Path unit that kidnapped you last year in Llata.'

Bruce and Jan glanced at each other. 'Is that so?' Bruce said. 'How do you know it was us?'

'You were with your son,' Jorge replied evenly. 'We confiscated your automobile. We also took a movie projector from you and some films on the life of Jesus.'

Jorge Rios suddenly commanded Bruce and Jan Benson's full attention. The couple asked more questions. Jorge, not a talkative young man by nature, answered them guardedly. He instinctively distrusted strangers. He would not have answered the Bensons' questions at all, in fact, except that Ruben Matías trusted the couple and Jorge trusted Matías with his life. The more he talked with Bruce and Jan, the more Jorge revealed of himself. Eventually, they learned his entire story.

*   *   *

From a young age, I experienced deep emotions that later led me to believe in Marxism. I come from a peasant family, raised in the jungle near Iquitos, the eldest of seven children. My father was a carpenter who built boats, an honest, hard-working man who could not seem to get ahead. I worked for years at my father's side, earning half wages to help support my younger brothers and sisters. My father's brother was just the opposite. He was a rich man. He owned a *hacienda*, a cattle ranch and a sugar mill. My father was his hired hand. I remember once when I was nine years old, I ate some oranges from my uncle's orchard. Later, Papa told me that I shouldn't eat them because my uncle took the cost of the oranges out of his salary. That broke my heart. This tremendous difference between the haves and the have-nots created in me a rebellious attitude. I set a personal goal: never, ever would I be exploited or humiliated by anybody.

At age 17, I entered the army. Since I had not gone to school, a military career was the only way I might someday get a job in a good business and earn decent wages. I was an airborne commando in Lima, graduating among the top ten in my class in weaponry skills and combat strategy. Based on that, the army recommended me for officers training school. I signed the papers and waited a month for my orders. None came, so I left the base and returned home to Iquitos.

I was 19 years old and had great expectations for success. Then I discovered that my mom had run off with another man, abandoning my brothers and sisters. The youngest, Eloy, was only four. Imagine seeing your family split up – one with grandmother, another with an uncle, another with a cousin – and my father crying himself to sleep every night. These things marked my life. Twice I tried to kill my mother and her boyfriend. In order not to do something crazy, I left town on a boat bound for Pucallpa.

I took to drinking. I sold what clothes I had to buy drugs. I joined street thieves and lived on what I stole. I slept under the trees. After some time, I went on to Tingo María, a town in the Upper Huallaga Valley where cocaine is produced. There I met a fellow who worked in drug trafficking and started working with him. I soon bought my own homestead on the Aguaytía River in the department of San Martín. In two or three years, the farm was producing several acres of coca leaf. I had my own laboratory to manufacture cocaine base. I started making a lot of money but it was a hazardous life. Although I had everything I wanted – money, women, friends – I couldn't find any meaning.

* * *

Jorge's lifestyle changed drastically when he joined Shining Path. He immediately abstained from drugs, alcohol and sex. He stopped making cocaine base and turned over his assets to the revolution. He no longer cared about making money. He wanted only to be the best revolutionary that he could be, because the Path embodied ideals of equality and justice for which Jorge longed. 'One objective united us all, to extend the revolution in our country,' he explained. 'Mao said that anyone who was unwilling to leave father and mother and all he possessed was incapable of inciting revolution in the earth.'

Mao would not have said that about Jorge. He was no mediocre militant. Jorge gave all that Shining Path demanded: absolute, unquestioning obedience. In some instances, that meant killing people, like the man he once publicly strangled to death on orders from his commanding officer. The victim, one of three condemned to die for violating revolutionary law, told Jorge that he was a Christian and that his life was 'safeguarded'. Jorge did not know what that meant, nor did he understand why the man kept uttering, 'Father, forgive them' all the while that Jorge twisted the rope tighter around his throat until the man spoke no more.

Jorge's loyalty to the Path endured every test. There was the night, for example, when his unit settled down in front of a movie screen to view the films they had confiscated from Bruce Benson in Llata. The films graphically depicted the life and death of Jesus. Seeing them moved several guerrillas to question the Marxist–Leninist–Maoist doctrine of Presidente Gonzalo. A few even decided to leave the guerrilla battalion. But not Jorge. His obedience to the Path was immovable.

Frequently, the Path demanded that Jorge kill people in uniform. His battalion ambushed police stations and military convoys. To mount such attacks, the *senderistas* divided themselves into two companies, the firing line and the assault team. The former group, by far the largest, commenced the attack by firing on the enemy with automatic weapons, rocket launchers and grenades. The small assault team waited until the barrage cut down some of the enemy, then moved in to confiscate the dead men's weapons. This was, of course, extremely dangerous. Only the most dedicated guerrillas volunteered for the assault team since the chances were great that they would die in the fight. As often as he could, Jorge Rios volunteered for the assault team.

One day his battalion ambushed a police convoy. Within minutes, the firing line cut down 25 men in uniform. Most of the dead lay in the back of an open truck, sitting on the road-side 60 feet below the *senderista* position. The assault team hesitated to go for the weapons. The only way down to the truck was hand-over-hand along a rope cast over the steep embankment. Even the most dedicated revolutionary thought twice about making the descent under enemy fire. Jorge did not hesitate, even though he had been assigned to the firing line that day. Handing his rifle to a comrade, he flung himself over the embankment and shinned down the rope and onto the police truck. Bullets flew in all directions, from the police officers concealed in the brush across the highway as well as from his own battalion above. Yet none hit Jorge. As he plundered the dead men of guns and ammunition, he raised a rifle in the air and shouted to his amazed comrades: 'Long live the Communist Party!'

Any guerrilla who survived such assaults gained hero status among his comrades and, sometimes, a promotion up the ranks. A week after this assault, Jorge's superiors promoted him to commander of a battalion of 280 guerrillas. The unit was headquartered in San Jorge, a village three miles into the jungle from Tingo María. Now, it was Jorge who gave orders to kill people who violated revolutionary law. He did not hesitate to do his duty.

Sometimes, Jorge gave orders to kill people in uniform. One day in October 1989, his unit ambushed a police convoy on the road near Tingo María. It turned out to be Jorge's last ambush. While reloading his automatic weapon, a rocket skimmed past his head and exploded on a tree branch five feet behind him, spraying Jorge with shrapnel. His comrades carried him from the battle to a clandestine clinic in the jungle. Doctors there managed to staunch the haemorrhaging and remove some of the shrapnel. Jorge would have to lie low in San Jorge for several weeks to recover, they said. His battalion assigned a bodyguard named Efraín to keep an eye on Jorge until he could get back on his feet. With time, his battle wounds healed. But now he suffered from a chronic headache. The headache had a name: Ruben Matías, pastor of the Christian and Missionary Alliance Church.

Normally when we entered a town, we gave three options to religious workers: join us, leave town within 24 hours, or be shot for resisting. A lot of religious workers died that way. When I returned to San Jorge to recuperate, the political officer of our battalion complained to me that Pastor Ruben Matías was still preaching the gospel. He would preach 'first God, then the Party'. For those of us who had given our lives to the revolution, that remark was a harsh blow to our convictions.

So I assigned some people to investigate this pastor in

order to find some serious fault in him – an incident of fraud, a theft, something that went against what he preached. We could not invent charges against him because that would go against our convictions. Furthermore, the pastor was blind and it was against the principles of the Path to kill the handicapped without just cause. When the investigators came back, they said they could find no crimes. In fact, the pastor was very much loved in the town.

He kept preaching. I often talked with Efraín about Pastor Matías. We tried to determine what to do about him. Everybody said I should eliminate him. It was dangerous having him around. We feared communism would lose its credibility with the people. He counselled a lot of the locals and, even though he was blind, he never asked a thing from anyone. He even knew communist ideology and would share informed opinions in our people's meetings.

One time I called a meeting to execute a fellow in San Jorge. A member of Pastor Matías's congregation was present. I asked if anyone had a word to say in favour of the condemned. A hand went up and this Christian man said, 'Why don't we give him another chance? Then, if he doesn't change, we can shoot him.' I asked him if he were willing to give his own life as a guarantee and he said yes. The majority of those who offered themselves as guarantors to keep us from executing people were Christians. On account of them, people converted to the gospel and stopped committing offences.

In one meeting in which Pastor Matías's wife and several members of his church were present, I decided to threaten him. I stood up in the middle of the group, pulled out my revolver and said: 'If I saw God Himself here right now, I'd blow off His head with this gun. Tell that pastor not to preach the gospel around here anymore. After all, this is a red zone. You all quit talking about God, or I'm going over there and set off a bomb in the middle of your worship service.'

Time passed and the pastor kept on with his meetings. I got angry. I told my officers, 'Call the town together, take them all into the jungle and bring the pastor. We are going to kill him.' I went and stood with my bodyguard Efraín beside a bridge, just a big log, really, and watched the people pass over on their way to the meeting. After a while, I saw Ruben Matías coming with his wife. I watched closely to see how this blind pastor was going to cross that big log. I watched and watched and, when he was ten feet away, I said, 'Hello, Pastor.'

'Hello. Who is speaking to me?'

'It's me, the battalion commander.'

'We're on our way to the meeting, eh?' he said. 'But I don't understand why they have me tied up. I think they must want to kill me.'

In that moment, I honestly think God intervened. I just stood there, watching him. In about 20 seconds, I made the decision.

'Well, Pastor, you can go back home with your wife.'

'Ah, okay, that's fine.' He turned around and left.

Efraín said, 'Okay, so tell me why we are having this meeting if the object was to kill the pastor?'

'Fine,' I said, 'give the order that the meeting is cancelled and everybody can go back home.'

There, in the company of those guerrillas, I realized deep down that I was a slave. Living for communism no longer satisfied me. But I could not withdraw, either. Once you join the Main Force, you cannot resign.

The security forces probably would not have captured Jorge Rios had he not violated his Shining Path convictions. Jorge was returning alone to San Jorge from a visit to a neighbouring battalion when he met Badd Araujo on the trail. Araujo was dressed in revolutionary chic – all black. He raised his hand in salute to Jorge. 'Hello, Comrade Commander.'

Caramba, this fellow knows me, Jorge thought to himself. 'Who are you?' he said to Araujo. 'What battalion are you with?'

'I'm from a battalion you do not know, a very powerful one. Even though they killed our commanding officer, he rose from the dead.'

Before Jorge knew what was happening, Araujo had produced a Bible from his rucksack and was reading texts of scripture that talked about Jesus and the Kingdom of God. When he finished, he said, 'According to the Bible, only the bravest will enter the Kingdom of God. Tell me, Comrade, are you brave enough to ask Jesus into your heart right here?'

Jorge thought a moment. 'No problem,' he said at length. 'What do I have to do?' This man in black was a nuisance and Jorge was prepared to do anything to rid himself of the fellow.

Araujo had Jorge kneel on the trail and repeat a prayer of confession, asking God to forgive his sins and grant him eternal life. They stood, Araujo embraced Jorge and said that the two of them were now brothers in Christ. Jorge didn't say anything.

'You know Pastor Ruben Matías, don't you?' Araujo asked.

'Yes, I do,' Jorge answered, startled.

'Every time I go to his house, he talks about you. He prays for you every day. Pastor Matías loves you very much.'

Then Badd Araujo was gone and Jorge stood alone on the trail. A feeling of great shame came over him. What a ridiculous spectacle he had made of himself. He, a Shining Path commander, kneeling to pray on a jungle trail with a Christian evangelist. He earnestly hoped no one found out about this. It would ruin his credibility as a communist. Prayer went completely against his Marxist convictions.

As so often happens, one compromise led to another. Five days later, a drug dealer with whom he had become acquainted invited Jorge to Tingo María to drink beer with a group of friends. Jorge accepted, although this also went against his Marxist convictions. The drug dealer found a discreet, secluded tavern. He understood that *senderistas* had to be careful whenever they ventured outside their red zone. For his part, Jorge suspected nothing unusual, even when the dealer abruptly excused himself and left the tavern. He understood that traffickers often had dealings that took them away at odd times. He was only beginning to feel a bit uneasy when, several minutes later, he heard behind his back the click of army rifles and a crisp, military command: 'Halt! Stay right where you are.'

They bound and blindfolded me and I spent the next several days like that in the stockade. It seems the soldiers confused me with one of my friends, because they tortured him more than me. I could hear his screams. I talked with my friend through a small hole in the wall between our cells and he told me the military knew that I was a guerrilla. After several days of torture, they sentenced me to the firing squad.

It was 10 o'clock in the evening when the duty officer told me I would be shot the next morning. I began reflecting on my life, my childhood, my adolescence, my friends, the guerrilla war. I felt so alone in that stockade. We had gone days without food, bound and blindfolded the whole time. Tears began to flow. Then I recalled the words of Pastor Matías, that in the most difficult moments, if you call out to God with all your heart, He is not slow to answer. It was impossible for me to believe in God. I heard my friend tapping on the wall. 'What are we going to do?' he asked. I said, 'The only solution is God.' When the early hours of the morning came, I had to face reality. I fell to the floor weeping and said, 'God, if you exist, I'm asking you to give me one more chance.'

That remark broke my heart. I realized everything I had ever done was all wrong and I did not know how to make it right. I did what Pastor Matías said to do, I asked God for forgiveness. I tried to anyway, best as I knew how. The pain was so strong I lost track of how long I was on the floor weeping. Afterward, it seemed as though I awoke from a dream. I stood up and discovered that the chains on my hands had fallen off and the blindfold had slipped from my eyes. I experienced a sudden and strange peace. My body felt anaesthetized. It was as if someone had lifted a thousand pounds off me. Dawn came, a military officer opened the door of my cell and asked, 'What happened to you? And who unbound you?'

The officer ordered Jorge bound and blindfolded once more, then loaded on the back of an army truck. As far as he knew, Jorge was on his way to his execution. Yet he felt such overwhelming peace that he was not afraid to die. He did not know that a commission of human rights inspectors had arrived from Lima that very morning to check the military stockade for torture victims. As a result, the soldiers were not taking him before a firing squad, but to the police station across town to hide him from the investigators. The army left instructions with the police chief that, unless he received an arrest order signed by a judge, he could keep Jorge just three days.

No such order arrived and three days later, Jorge walked out of the jail and back to San Jorge, where he dawdled about for five days, trying to determine what to do. He finally decided he must talk with Ruben Matías.

Jorge knocked on the pastor's door early one morning. 'Who's there?' a voice called from inside the house.

'Jorge Rios. May I talk to you, please?'

The pastor's daughter, Janeth, opened the door, her eyes wide with alarm. 'Well . . . come in,' she stammered, her gaze fixed on the revolver stuck in Jorge's belt. Janeth had good reason for alarm. This was, after all, the man who not long ago had threatened to set off a bomb in her father's church. Nevertheless, she invited him to stay for breakfast.

Jorge talked with Ruben Matías for the entire morning. He told the pastor of his experience in the stockade. 'I came here intending to accept Christ into my life,' he said. 'I don't want to be the same person any more. I don't feel like the same person any more. I know there is something I need to do.'

Matías advised Jorge to confirm his decision to follow Christ, voluntarily and from the heart. They prayed. Matías had Jorge listen to a taped recording of Nicky Cruz, who told of his conversion to Christ while leading a street gang in New York City. Jorge found the account quite moving, particularly because, like Cruz, his conversion to Christ put him in serious jeopardy with his former comrades.

'Where do I go?' he asked Matías. 'Once the guerrillas find out I've become a Christian, I won't be able to remain here in the red zone.'

Despite the risks, Jorge had no intention of hiding his Christianity. The next Sunday he attended worship at the Christian and Missionary Alliance Church and, at the invitation of the pastor, publicly confirmed his faith in Christ. Word of the battalion commander's decision spread quickly through San Jorge. A few days later, a band of guerrillas on motorcycles surrounded Jorge at a bus stop and told him to come with them. He knew it was no good arguing. He did ask that they allow him to say goodbye to Ruben Matías, who just at that moment was arriving on a bus from Tingo María. Jorge briefly explained to the sightless pastor what was happening.

'If I can, I will try to escape,' Jorge said, tears welling up in his eyes.

Matías sighed. 'Don't be afraid,' he said. 'You are a Christian. Even if they kill you, you are in the Kingdom of God.' Matías slipped a New Testament and a bit of cash into Jorge's rucksack before the young man roared off on the back of a motorcycle.

The commander of the guerrilla battalion that captured Jorge was an old friend, so he did not order his prisoner bound. In fact, the commander tried his best to put Jorge at ease, acting as though the Path had no intention of killing him. Jorge knew very well the Path intended to kill him, but out of regard for his friend, acted as though he suspected nothing. The charade eventually put the commander at ease, so much so, in fact, that when Jorge asked to return to town to collect a debt, the man agreed, assigning two guerrillas to escort him. Jorge realized the two were novice guerrillas when they accepted his invitation to stop for beer on the way into town. While they drank, Jorge excused himself to go to the bathroom. From there, he slipped out the back of the tavern and into the jungle. Late that night, he made his way to Ruben Matías's house.

Matías's relief at seeing Jorge was tempered by some distressing news he had just received. The army was looking for Jorge again. This time they had obtained an arrest warrant, signed by a judge. If he were caught this time, no human rights inspectors would save him. Matías had a plan, however. He would organize an underground escape route to Lima, using contacts with fellow pastors who lived along the way. Meanwhile, Jorge could hide out in an upstairs storage room at the Assembly of God Church in Tingo María. The army would not look for him there because the church stood but a block away from the police station. Only Ruben Matías and the pastor of the Assembly of God Church knew of the plan. Jorge would be safe as long as he stayed out of sight. He did stay out of sight in the second floor storage room for several days. Then one morning he slipped out to get some breakfast, having passed those several days with little to eat. Five seconds after he emerged onto the street, a police truck pulled up, several officers jumped out and arrested him.

Now Ruben Matías used his contacts with fellow pastors to seek clemency for Jorge. One by one, evangelical ministers sought interviews with the police chief to speak on behalf of the captured guerrilla. *Ex*-guerrilla, they emphasized, pointing out that Jorge was now on Shining Path's death list, due to his conversion to Christ. If the Path was seeking to kill him as a traitor, should not the authorities grant him amnesty? The police responded to this argument by raiding the Assembly of God Church and threatening to close it down for harbouring a subversive. The officers also threatened to arrest the pastors who came to seek clemency for Jorge Rios. Badd Araujo even suffered blows at the hands of the officers, who gave him 12 hours to leave Tingo María, or else.

Their harsh treatment notwithstanding, the police actually saved Jorge's life by arresting him before the army did. Military officers insisted the prisoner be surrendered to them to face a firing squad. The police chief resisted the demand, perhaps because he relished the prospect of liquidating a notorious *senderista* himself. Once, when he had had too much to drink, he came to Jorge's cell brandishing his revolver. 'You see this pistol?' he cackled. 'You will be the sixth person put to death with this gun.'

The final card God had left to play for me was Pastor Ruben Matías. He went and asked to speak with the police chief. 'Are you, too, here on account of that guerrilla?' the officer said.

'No, I've come on your account, Commander. We have a lot to discuss with regard to the gospel, because you, sir, are a sinner, just as I am.'

'You, sir, as well as Jorge, are equally lost persons,' the pastor said. 'Nevertheless, Christ loves you both. He wants you both for himself. That's why, sir, you have no right to kill that young man. Only God can pass sentence on his life.'

Pastor Matías preached Christ to the police chief in such a way that he was touched by God. He described my conversion to Christ and asked the officer to do what was right. Then he left. Two days later, the police chief came and stood at my cell door for two whole minutes without saying a word. I finally stood up and he motioned for me to come over to him. I could see that he had tears in his eyes.

'Why did you become a guerrilla?' he said. 'I have two sons of my own, and I would never want them to be in the position that you are in now. Look, I have here an order to liquidate you.'

'Everything you know about me is true,' I said. I confessed things I had never before confessed to any military officer or policeman. 'It's true that I was a terrorist. I did this and that thing. But I've surrendered my life to Christ. Maybe this has no meaning to you, but I can truly say that I do not fear what you can do with my life.'

'Don't worry,' he said. 'Your pastor spoke with me and we came to an agreement. From this moment on, you are officially dead.' He took out my arrest file, tore it into pieces and set it afire.

'Look, I can't release you here,' he said. 'Either the military or the guerrillas will kill you. However, I have this warrant from the army for your arrest. The charge is desertion of post.'

The arrest warrant was for that episode when the army recommended me for officers school. Thinking I had not been accepted, I left base after a month of waiting, just when the order came for me to report to the school. When the base officer couldn't find me, he reported me for desertion.

The police chief told me he was turning me over to the military in Lima. 'As a guerrilla, you are hereby terminated. We are erasing your entire file. Tomorrow, you go to the capital by plane.'

'I have never done this for any prisoner,' he added, 'even worse, for a prisoner like yourself. To be honest, what your pastor told me about God truly moved me. What moved me even more was that you are nothing to him, not a son, not even a relative. Yet he persisted in seeking clemency for you, even at risk of implicating himself as a Shining Path sympathizer.'

The police chief fixed his eyes on me. 'I hope you will be a real Christian,' he said. 'I hope your life has truly been changed.'

The next morning, escorted by two police officers, I flew to Lima in a military plane. They delivered me to the Palace of Justice and, three days later, I was transferred to the military stockade. After two weeks, Pastor Matías found me there. Wilfredo Castro, pastor of the Christian and Missionary Alliance Church in Chorrillos, paid my fine for the desertion charges and the military freed me.

*   *   *

Jorge had gained his freedom only days before meeting Bruce and Jan Benson at the luncheon in Chorrillos. That was why the young man was still suspicious of strangers, thinking they might betray him to the security forces or, worse, to the Path. Despite his suspicions, Jorge answered all the Bensons' questions about the incident in Llata, which had taken place just one year, almost to the day, before their lunch together.

'Tell me, what did the Path intend to do with us?' Bruce asked.

Rios looked at the floor. 'We had orders to kill you. But we didn't, or rather, we couldn't. Something prevented us from carrying out the orders.'

The Bensons glanced at each other. For an instant, they relived the terror of their capture on that lonely mountain road and then the inexplicable peace that had settled over them as the day wore on. 'Jorge, it was not "something" that prevented you, it was Someone,' Bruce said gently. 'We felt God had placed His angels around us that day.'

Jorge pondered this before filling in the details. The Path's military command had instructed the guerrillas to eliminate all outsiders they encountered. Shining Path wanted the area purged of everyone but local residents. Once the people's meeting in the town square had ended, the *senderistas* were to take the Benson family to a secluded spot outside town where their bodies would not easily be found and execute them.

'But before we could carry out the order, we received a radio communication that the army was closing in on Llata,' Jorge said. 'We did not know, however, if they were ahead or behind us, so we had to withdraw hastily. We had no time to carry out the order.'

A momentary silence hung over the Bensons and their new acquaintance. From what they had just learned of Jorge and his former comrades, Bruce and Jan did not doubt they would have carried out the order to the letter, had they not been forced to run from the army. Strange thing about the army, though. The Bensons saw no military activity anywhere near Llata the entire fortnight they spent in the village.

Jorge broke the silence. 'You know, I have done a lot of bad things in my life,' he said. 'I'm just now beginning to realize how much pain and suffering I've caused people like you, and I want to say something, now that I have the chance.'

He rose to his feet. 'I'm sorry,' he said. 'Can you ever find it in your hearts to forgive me?'

7

Exodus in the
Time of Troubles

The inexorable advance of Shining Path down the Ene and
Tambo Rivers left Ashaninka communities reeling from the
effects. 'Liberation' brought death, bondage and hunger to the
native villages. When the Path arrived in Puerto Ashaninka, a
town near the confluence of the Ene and Tambo Rivers, they
forced the villagers to gather for the customary people's meeting. The *senderistas* expounded the Marxist–Leninist–Maoist
doctrine of Presidente Gonzalo and told the Ashaninka that,
now that theirs was a liberated community, they were expected
to cooperate with the revolution. Amiel Ernesto spoke up to say
that he did not intend to cooperate with the revolution because
its doctrine went against the teachings of the Word of God.

The *senderistas* had heard this objection before and decided
they must make an example of the impertinent young man.
They hauled Amiel in front of the assembly and stabbed him to
death while his wife, Angela, and Amiel's three-year-old son
watched helplessly. The rest of the villagers were helpless to
defend Amiel. The *senderistas* had been careful to take away
their shotguns, bows and arrows before the meeting began.
The only option open to the villagers now was to cooperate with
the revolution or die as Amiel had. The entire village, including
Amiel's parents and his eight younger brothers and sisters,
resigned themselves to submission. That meant they had to
abandon their thriving coffee and cocoa farms to live as virtual
slaves of the Path. For the next three years, the villagers of
Puerto Ashaninka wandered from one clandestine guerrilla
base to another, growing rice and beans for the *senderistas*.
They themselves ate what they could forage in the jungle and

what the Path allowed them to eat of the crops they grew for the revolution. In other words, they ate very little.

Shining Path constantly preached the themes of equality and justice to the Ashaninka. Nevertheless, the natives never fully grasped the connection between the revolution and those lofty principles. In fact, the Ashaninka customarily referred to the years of the late 1980s and early 1990s as 'the Troubles'. The Ashaninka who lived in the Satipo area suffered the most during the revolution. The Path plundered and burned scores of villages there, liquidating villagers who resisted liberation and herding the survivors into concentration camps.

When Maurine Friesen talks about the Troubles, her blue eyes fairly blaze. 'There were a lot of children killed in this whole thing. It was terrible. I mean, the Path was cruel.'

For Maurine, the cruellest crime Shining Path committed against the Ashaninka was to force them to take up arms against their own people. Many, at first, refused to do so and saw their own families murdered. Then, with terrorist guns at their backs, the survivors were ordered to attack neighbouring communities. Ashaninka women and children served as the shock troops in these invasions, swarming into a village to loot houses and set them afire. Ashaninka men would follow, attacking with arrows and machetes. Finally, armed terrorists would emerge from the bush to mop up remaining resistance.

The Friesens believe that between 1,000 and 1,500 Ashaninka died in the Troubles. That means the Path destroyed 5 per cent of the tribe. Perhaps those casualty figures do not seem so terrible to outsiders. Yet, had Shining Path inflicted the same quantity of suffering on the entire Republic of Peru, the war would not have claimed just 25,000 lives, but 850,000.

*   *   *

Mrs Natividad Aranibar Cecilio is having a quiet morning in Puerto Ocopa. Her six eldest children are at school and she is home alone with three-year-old Pablo Cecilio. The toddler was named after Natividad's husband, who once pastored the Ashaninka Evangelical Church in Alto Gloriabamba. That was before the Troubles forced Natividad and her young family to leave Alto Gloriabamba and come to live in Puerto Ocopa.

Mrs Cecilio's home is typical Ashaninka. A chest-high hedge surrounds the compound, which is located next door to the identical compound of her uncle, Diego Quichaite. Scattered banana palms and papaya trees grow out of hard-packed earth within the enclosure. Three separate buildings, all of cane walls and palm roofs, provide living quarters. One building is for sleeping, the kitchen occupies another. The largest serves as a combination dining hall and work room. Fish nets hang from the rafters here. Natividad sits at a long table of rough-hewn planks and recounts the saga of her struggle to bring her family through the Troubles.

The *senderistas* came for the first time in June at 8 o'clock in the evening. The family had already retired for the night. They were about 30 terrorists. Villagers from Gloriabamba, Ashaninka as am I, were with them. They called out to my husband, Pablo. 'Uncle, uncle, you have visitors.'

'By any chance, do soldiers come around here?' the *senderistas* asked him.

'What soldiers would come here?' Pablo said. 'No one comes round here but the coffee buyers.'

'If you see soldiers, you will let us know,' they said. I think that was just a pretext. The neighbours in Gloriabamba had told the Path, 'Did you know that one of our neighbours wants to organize a civilian militia?' But we knew nothing of any such civilian militia.

I stayed in bed with the children that night. The next morning I asked my husband, 'Who were those people who came here last night?'

'They were villagers from Gloriabamba. There was also an outsider,' he replied.

'Why did they come?'

'They want us to support them, so they can be the "new generation". They said we are going to have our own markets. One day we will have big shops, like the outsiders.'

'What are they going to do?'

'I don't know. I don't understand very well what the Path is.'

Later I discovered that the Path wanted to kill my husband. It was due to their jealousy because of the 20 acres of coffee that we owned. Also, my husband was the pastor of the Ashaninka Evangelical church in our community, a congregation of 15 members.

One day we were harvesting beans and a helicopter passed by, flying quite low to the ground. It was the mayor, Santiago Contoricón, making a tour of the communities. I called out, 'Come down, Santiago! Land your helicopter here!' That afternoon, the *senderistas* came back, along with the villagers of Gloriabamba.

'Auntie, has a helicopter passed by here?' they asked me.

'Yes, it passed.'

'Tell us, did it land? Did you see it land?'

'No, it passed on and went to Satipo.'

They said to my husband: 'It would be better if you left your house and made a hut for yourself in the jungle. Then, when the helicopter comes, no one is going to go out and signal it.' Later, they took my husband aside to speak to him. When they finished he came back rather sad and quickly began to collect his clothing.

'Where are you going?' I said.

'I am going with them,' he replied.

'Why?'

'Because if I don't, they will kill me.'

'And what about me? Where will I go?' I had my three-month-old son and did not know what to do.

'Go to your uncle,' he replied. 'And pray for me. I have no idea what they will do.'

After three days, my husband came back. He said the *senderistas* had taken him to Villarrica. In mid-journey, they suddenly grabbed hold of him and said: 'Are you going to escape, or do you want to go make salt fish?' Pablo did not know what they meant by 'make salt fish'. We later learned it was their way of referring to a massacre.

'Why would I want to escape?' he said to them.

'Do you have children, 14 years or older?' they asked.

'No, they are all ten years or younger.'

'Well, then, do you have a gun?'

'Yes, I do.'

'Why did you buy it?'

'For game, to hunt in the jungle.'

'By any chance, is your shotgun for killing us?'

'No. It is not for killing people. It is for game, so that my children can have meat.'

'Your shotgun is not for people, eh? We will see.' They continued walking.

When they reached Villarrica, the *senderistas* took away all the villagers' clothing and burned down their houses. My husband stood there watching and wondering why they were doing this. He saw the villagers escape into the jungle, making for Palomar. Later, an Ashaninka told him that the *senderistas* had captured the school teacher and killed him. My husband did not see it. They took the teacher to the river and killed him with a knife. The water carried the body away.

After this, the Path started coming frequently to Gloriabamba to hold meetings. They elected a directorate and a secretary. 'My boss says everybody now is going to change their name,' the secretary said. 'From the smallest baby to the most elderly.'

I said, 'Why? I already have a name, "Natividad". It is enough for me.' (Well, Pablo sometimes called me by the intimate nickname 'Martha', but I didn't tell the secretary about that.)

'But you must change your name,' he insisted. 'If you don't, I will have to address you in a different way.'

I think this was his way of saying they were going to kill me if I didn't obey. We gave the directorate some *masato* and it put them in a cheerful mood.

In February, they told us that Comrade Roberto, a commander of the Path, was going to arrive. Right away, Pablo took me to fetch manioc and beans. 'If we harvest these beans, are we going to sell them?' I asked him.

'No.'

'We had better leave this coffee farm once and for all,' I said gloomily. 'Let's go to Mazamari. Let's escape with our children.'

'Ay, no! We can't do that!' Pablo said. 'The Path has armed guerrillas on the roads, watching them all the time. If they see us, they will kill us. God knows, we are going to die in this jungle.'

When I returned to the house, I found my children screaming and crying. My house was surrounded by *senderistas* and villagers from Gloriabamba, all armed. They were examining Pablo's shotgun, which they had removed from the storage chest. I thought they were going to kill my son. 'What's going on?' I said to them.

'Ah, Auntie, good morning.'

'Good morning.'

Comrade Roberto came up to me. I saw many armed guerrillas down the hill. 'Auntie, you have a shotgun, don't you? I would like you to loan it to me,' he said.

At that moment my husband arrived. 'Uncle, let's go over there and talk,' the man said, and three of them took Pablo aside.

My son was frightened. 'Mama, that one took a shotgun shell,' he said. 'What are they going to do?' I opened the storage chest and it was empty. They had taken out everything – shells, casings, gunpowder – everything that was in there.

Roberto told my husband, 'If you don't want to fight, it's better that you give me your gun. And if you don't have children to defend the revolution, you must come with me yourself. Why are you staying at home?'

The next week, they came and took my husband away to build a hut in the jungle. Later a *senderista* came with two villagers to take me and the family away. 'The house your husband has been building is ready now,' they said. 'The rest of the married women are already there, expecting you.'

I packed up all the children's clothes that were in the house. I hid my jewellery and buried my documents. I took my Bible and a book of hymns in my language. I had the man carry my son, because he could not yet walk. 'We are going to follow the ridges of the hills,' he told me. 'If we don't, the paratroopers will kill us. They do not allow anyone to travel the roads.'

I hope to God no one has killed my husband, I said in my heart. We were out there for one week. Then we went on to Alto Shankerani and descended to Saureni, where Pablo was living in a small hut.

'What are we going to do?' I asked Pablo one night. 'Here in this shack our children are going to die. We have no food, we have no manioc.' We could not grow food in Saureni, because in order to hide themselves in the bush, the *senderistas* did not allow us to clear farm plots.

'Look, my brother is in Puerto Ashaninka,' my husband said. 'I will say to Comrade Roberto that I am going there to prepare land, to get it ready to plant bananas for the Path. Let's see if I can trick Roberto.'

'Yes, trick him,' I said.

The next morning, Pablo spoke with Roberto. A few days later, the commander gathered everybody together and said: 'This family is going to prepare land in Puerto Ashaninka in order to plant bananas and sow beans for us to eat. It is good that they are going to support us with these crops.' In fact, we really wanted to escape from the hands of the Path.

'We don't want any believers here,' Shining Path had told us. 'We do not worship God. There is no God.' They did not allow prayers or worship. So we hid our Bibles. When Shining Path was not around, we read the Bible and sang hymns. We prayed every day. At night, when we lay down to sleep, we prayed in our little hut. We wanted to learn more about the Bible, especially the book of Exodus. We never told the *senderistas* what we were doing.

Shining Path had taken nearly four hundred villagers from Gloriabamba. Once we started living in the jungle, the people began dying off. Some spoke out against the Path and they killed them. Many died of colds or pneumonia or anaemia or cholera. One by one they died.

A woman who was not a believer asked me why my

children did not die.'Why, until now, has this anaemia not attacked them?' she asked.

'It is because we are believers,' I said.'Are you a believer?'

'No, no one has ever taught me.'

'Listen, there is only one God who has created us. We believe this One gives us children. When they are born, you must begin praying for them from the beginning.'

'You are right about that,' she said.'Of course, that's why your children are alive.'

But she continued to live as a pagan. She did not believe in God. Every one of her children died, just like the children of the other women. She herself finally died, too.

* * *

We stayed two months in Puerto Ashaninka. In April, the army formed a civilian militia with the people of Puerto Ocopa and surrounded us. The *senderistas* did not realize the soldiers were there in the jungle, waiting to capture us. They sent our band of women up to dig weeds out of a rice field. We were resting on the way and my children were looking for snails in the bush.'Come here!' I told them.'We are going to pray that when the soldiers come, God will not let them kill us. Let's pray.'

Somebody murmured,'What do you think you're doing?'

'I'm asking God to get us out of here.'

'That's good.'

It was not a half hour later that a companion of ours came up the road shouting,'The soldiers are coming! The soldiers are coming!'

'Shut up! Be quiet!' someone said.'Be still, sit down. If the soldiers were to come right now, they would strafe you all with machine-gun fire. They will kill all your husbands.'

The soldiers found us there. A captain was with them.'Is this all your people?' he asked.'Where are the others?'

'They are not here, officer,' I said. I was the only one who understood Spanish well, so I spoke for the rest of the women.

'And your husbands?'

'The Path took them away. A man ordered them to go up the Ene River to visit some young woman who wants to join the guerrillas. I don't know much about it.'

'Is that the truth?'

'That is the truth.'

'There was another woman in this group. Where is she?'

'She died, day before yesterday.'

'Are you lying to me?'

'No, officer, I do not lie. If you want to see for yourself, the cemetery is just over there.'

'What did she die of? Did they kill her?'

'No, they did not kill her. It was cholera. She turned black, all purple around the mouth. She had diarrhoea.'

'Ah yes, that is cholera,' he said. 'Where is your village?'

'My village is Alto Gloriabamba. Shining Path brought me here.'

'You were deceived, is that so?'

'Yes, we were all deceived. We knew nothing about the Path. No one warned us.'

'Are these your children?'

'Yes they are, all of them.'

'None have been taken from you?'

'Not one. But they took away some of the other women's children.'

'Okay, let's go.'

The soldiers tore down all the houses, tin roofs and all. The next day we left at six o'clock in the morning for Puerto Ocopa. The soldiers had left two long boats at the mouth of the Tambo River. We put all the little boys and girls and our rucksacks in the boats, in order to travel faster. For the march, we spread out, three women with two soldiers in between to guard us. We heard shooting and thought the captain and the children had been killed. An Ashaninka woman said to me, 'Let's escape! We must save ourselves.'

'Why should I escape?' I said. 'I want them to rescue me. I want to save my children. We will be safe over there with the soldiers. I once studied in Puerto Ocopa. I have an uncle there, my mother's brother.'

That afternoon, we arrived in Puerto Ocopa. My children had not seen their father, so they were weeping. 'What has happened to Papa?' they cried. 'When is Papa going to come?'

'I don't know,' I told them. 'We must ask God in prayer to help your papa get away from the Path. Let's pray.'

As she prayed, Natividad said in her heart: 'O Lord, you know that shooting we heard as we escaped Puerto Ashaninka? Please, Lord, don't let it be that Pablo was in the line of fire.'

* * *

On that April day, Pablo Cecilio was, in fact, a long way from the line of fire. He and the other Ashaninka men had marched a good distance up the Ene River with their Shining Path overlords. Several days passed before word reached them that the army had invaded Puerto Ashaninka. What is more, they heard a quite disturbing version of events from the Path.

'They have killed your families,' the messenger said. 'The soldiers deceived them. They killed your wives and all your children.'

Pablo Cecilio would not accept the shocking news. He took the messenger aside and questioned him directly about his family's fate.

'I was at the river when it happened,' the *senderista* said. 'The soldiers took the women there one by one and killed them. Afterward, they threw their bodies into the river.'

Pablo and his Ashaninka companions had little time to grieve their loss. 'Let's get going, we're heading for Alto Beni,' the *senderistas* ordered. They were anxious to clear out of the area. 'We are going toward Ayacucho. Get moving!'

The group set out on the trail. For several weeks, they made their way up the Ene and into the department of Ayacucho, where that river meets the Apurimac flowing down from the highlands. Day after day, Pablo contemplated the possibility that his family was gone. 'How could my wife and family be dead? If they were in the hands of the soldiers who rescued them, how could they have died?'

He concluded that he would not accept the Path's story about Puerto Ashaninka until he had discovered for himself what had happened. Pablo began to plan his escape. The first phase of his scheme was to feign a radical personality change. The alert coffee farmer and pastor transformed himself into a mute and passive foot-soldier. He obeyed orders from the Path automatically and without comment. The *senderistas* satisfied themselves that the lie about the massacre had succeeded in destroying the man's hopes. But the lie only reinforced Pablo's determination to get away from Shining Path once and for all. 'I have to surprise them with my escape,' he told himself. 'I must see my wife and children again.'

The group was nearing Ayacucho and the edge of the jungle when Pablo's chance came. 'Who's going to go fishing?' the *senderistas* asked one day. 'Cecilio, do you want to go?' The terrorists had come to respect Pablo's skill at taking fish from the river. They ate well when Cecilio went fishing.

Pablo shrugged. 'I'm used to it.'

'Go on then. Bring back plenty of fish for us.'

The *senderistas* knew Pablo would not try to run away, since the weeks of upriver trekking had brought them far from his home territory. They were right that Pablo would not run away. He had a different kind of escape in mind and that afternoon while fishing, he came upon the thing he needed: a *balsa*. A fellow Ashaninka had used the raft for a trip down river then, as was customary, discarded it along the bank. The trip had been a recent one. The *balsa* was intact, fit for another cruise. Pablo made sure no one saw him tying the raft securely to a tree and covering it with brush.

He prepared the next step in his plan later that evening while his companions were digesting their fish supper. He packed a few essential travel items – a change of clothing, string, a knife, matches – in a small rucksack and hid it in the brush between camp and the concealed *balsa*. The final step entailed the most risk. It came the following afternoon, when the *senderistas* distributed soap to the Ashaninka men and told them to go and bathe. Pablo took his time preparing for his bath. In fact, his companions barely noticed that he was still fully clothed after they had stripped and plunged into the water.

'Excuse me. I must go relieve myself,' he said.

He shuffled away into the bush. His companions splashed about, relishing a dip in the river. No need to hurry. They were in secure, *senderista*-controlled territory and could afford some leisure. Besides, a refreshing bath in the river was one of the few pleasures they enjoyed on their trek. By the time the bathers were back ashore, twilight was falling. It was then, while they dried themselves and dressed, that someone asked: 'Where is Pablo Cecilio?'

Pablo had sauntered off a short way into the jungle, just out of sight of his companions, then broke into a dead run. He came to the place where his pack lay hidden, scooped up the bundle and kept running. When he was far down river, he plunged into the water. Pablo swam along with the current to the spot where the *balsa* lay hidden, cut the tethers and pushed the raft into midstream. By then, it was around 6 p.m. and thick, tropical darkness was beginning to envelop the jungle. The fugitive lay down on his tiny craft and gulped deep breaths. He prayed, 'Please, Lord, don't let them see me.'

All that night, Pablo lay on the *balsa* as the river carried him further away from his captors and closer to home. He floated most of the following day, as well. By then he had put enough distance between himself and the *senderistas* from whom he had fled that he began to believe his escape would succeed. Then, they saw him.

The guerrilla band camped on the riverbank caught sight of Pablo before he caught sight of them. He knew it foolish to try to escape, that would only arouse suspicion. He would have to use his wits. Pablo cheerfully hailed the terrorist commander. 'Good day, Comrade!'

'Good day.'

Pablo manoeuvred the raft to shore and faced the commander. He noted the man was quite drunk, and groggy as well, from an afternoon siesta.

'What can we do for you, Comrade?' the man mumbled.

'Nothing, thank you,' Pablo said. 'I'm fine. The comrades sent me down here to scout good fishing holes.'

'Where are you going to fish?'

'Just downstream a bit. Have you caught anything there?'

'No, nothing. Look, I've been drinking,' he said, tottering about on unstable legs. The *senderista* seemed eager to impress his new comrade. 'Here, let's give our friend some manioc,' he said to a woman in the group. Perhaps the man thought a gift might restrain Pablo from reporting his drunkenness, a quite unrevolutionary vice, to his commander. For whatever motive, Pablo was grateful for the manioc. In order not to attract attention, he had taken no food from his own camp.

'Thanks very much, Comrade,' Pablo said, and stuffed the manioc in his rucksack. 'I must be going now. I have only until tomorrow to rejoin my unit.'

'What time will you arrive?'

'I should meet them early in the morning. My comrades are on their way here now.' It was a lie, of course. Pablo hoped never to meet his 'comrades' again.

He left the guerrillas, floated a short way down river and ditched the *balsa*. It was probable that he would meet more terrorist cadres along the waterway, but unlikely that other Shining Path commanders would be so agreeably intoxicated. He struck out through the bush, avoiding the trail that wound along the river bank. For days he walked, following the ridges of the lush foothills and calculating the most direct route between himself and Alto Gloriabamba. He saw no other human being. One afternoon he climbed a tree and spotted the broad Tambo off in the distance. He knew from the lie of the land that he was still many days away from home. He had eaten very little during the march except for fruits and edible herbs he stumbled across in his wanderings. Manioc cannot be eaten raw and Pablo could not cook the manioc he carried in his rucksack without a fire. One night, he managed to capture a partridge. He dressed it and was dining on the raw flesh when it suddenly occurred to him that he had put matches in his rucksack before fleeing. He rummaged through the bag until he found them. 'Well, I have matches,' he said, smiling. 'And I have manioc. At least I'm not going to starve.'

Pablo reached his house in Alto Gloriabamba several days

later but found no one home. He had hoped Natividad and the children would be there, but he could see that no one had set foot on the property since he left it more than a year before. That meant that if his family were still alive, they would be in Puerto Ocopa with the army. Pablo would have to go there to look for them.

However, this posed a serious risk. The army knew Pablo Cecilio had been with the Path for several months. In the army's eyes, that made him a *senderista*. The army shot *senderistas* on sight. Well, that was a risk he was going to have to take if he wanted ever to see his family again. He prayed, then set out. On a Saturday, one month after his escape from Shining Path, Pablo arrived on a hilltop overlooking Puerto Ocopa.

*   *   *

The refugees from Puerto Ashaninka were quartered in the Catholic mission in Puerto Ocopa. The soldiers had converted the old brick and stone structure into barracks because it could be easily defended in the event of attack. And, it was the only building in town large enough to accommodate several hundred Ashaninka, mostly women and children. The soldiers wanted the refugees under one roof where they could keep an eye on them, just in case they took it in their heads to return to the Path. None did.

For more than six months, Mrs Natividad Cecilio and her six children lived in the refugee camp at Puerto Ocopa under the protection of the army. There on a November morning, the final chapter of their family saga unfolded. Natividad's large, brown eyes do not blink as she recalls it.

It was early on a Sunday. We were assembled for flag-raising when the soldier on guard duty came and called the sergeant.

'Sergeant, I don't know who, but somebody left this paper out there.'

The sergeant looked at the note. 'Some repentant *senderista* is about. Where did you find this?'

'Out there,' the soldier pointed. 'The terrorist has put up a white flag.'

'We better have a look. Go get that white flag and bring it here.'

Meanwhile, we were hoisting the flag and marching around the parade ground. The commander of the civilian militia came and asked me, 'Mrs Cecilio, does your husband know how to write?'

'Why?'

'We have a letter here that says: "I'm without clothing, drenched by the rain. I have been deceived and manipulated by Shining Path. But I managed to escape from their hands." By any chance, could your husband have written this?'

'Yes, he could have. Let me see the signature.'

'There is no signature, look.'

He showed me the letter. 'It looks like his handwriting,' I said. 'Oh yes! He's out there, he's out there!'

A group of men came marching into town. So many of the other refugees were milling about, I was unable to see who it was. The captain found me and said: 'Mrs Cecilio, come with me. We are going to see if you can identify this man.'

Just then a soldier I knew passed by.

'What's his name, the refugee's name?' I asked.

'Ah, I can't say. The sergeant did not give me his name.'

'Well, tell him to give you the name!'

At that moment, the troops passed by and there was Pablo, walking in the middle of them. 'Hello, Martha,' he said to me.

'Hello, Pablo.' We smiled at each other.

The captain said to me, '*Señora*, leave your husband first to me, and later you may come talk with him. Please, be ready when I call you.'

Both Pablo and I wept when we met again. The children, too, were so happy. God had answered our prayers. It was all joy.

8

Compelling Truth

In 1968, American missionary Norman Mydske founded Pacific Radio in Lima. The broadcasting station was named, logically, after the great ocean that lies off Peru's western coast. However, the name turned out to be prophetic, in the Old Testament sense, for Pacific Radio was destined to play a role in the pacification of Peru.

A decade after opening the station, Mydske left the mission field to become Latin America Director for the Billy Graham Evangelistic Association, leaving Pacific Radio in the hands of Pedro Ferreira. A decade after that, the Shining Path war was building to a violent apex when Ferreira envisioned the role that Pacific Radio could play in bringing peace to his troubled land.

'It suddenly occurred to us that, since we had a radio station, we ought to raise up a column of prayer,' Ferreira later told a journalist. 'What with the political violence, the economy in shambles and hazardous conditions all over Peru, we were living under tremendous stress. So on Sunday, 7 May 1989, at 6 o'clock in the morning, we began calling the church to pray before going to its places of worship.'

Pacific Radio's call to prayer built steady momentum. Eventually, some 50,000 Peruvians paused every Sunday morning to pray for their troubled nation. The prayer movement also spawned all-night vigils on Fridays. It finally gave birth to a Day of National Reconciliation, celebrated annually in Lima's soccer stadium.

'This national prayer movement really was born in the heart of God,' Ferreira said. 'There was no organization, no money, no strategy, just a call to pray. We believe, as Isaiah 58 says, that true fasting and prayer bring liberation. Walls come falling down, shackles are removed, blessing comes from God and takes away the curse.'

*   *   *

Early on 10 July 1993, Juan Mallea left the modest apartment in the Lima suburb of Comas that he shared with his wife Cristina and their nine-month-old son Juancito, without the slightest notion that he would not return home to them that evening. A taxi driver by vocation, Juan picked up his first fare of the day, a neighbour named Juan Jara, who asked to be taken to an apartment complex ten minutes away. Jara asked Mallea to wait for him while he visited a friend in the building. Jara never got inside. Several strangers answered the door and immediately seized him. Other strangers walked up to Mallea's waiting cab.

'We are investigators from the anti-terrorist intelligence service,' they said. 'We want to ask you some questions.'

Juan said he would be glad to answer their questions, although he knew nothing about terrorism. He did not know, for example, that the apartment building housed suspected terrorists, whom the intelligence officers had been keeping under surveillance. Nor did he know the investigators suspected Jara of having ties to Shining Path. Could they search his taxi? Of course, Juan said. He had nothing to hide. They searched and found nothing, except Juan's Bible. Could they search his home? Of course, Juan said, and led the strangers back to his modest apartment. They searched it, but found nothing. Nevertheless, they said, Juan would have to come with them to the National Directorate Against Terrorism, DINCOTE as it was known, so they could conduct a thorough background check. He could expect to be there about three days. That would be fine, Juan said. He wanted to cooperate fully with the investigation so that the authorities could satisfy themselves that he knew nothing about terrorism. He kissed Juancito and Cristina, who was four months pregnant with their second child, and left with the strangers.

The first days in the holding cell at DINCOTE, Juan maintained his composure, despite having to share the space with more than 60 other men, half of whom knew quite a lot about terrorism. Many of the men were undergoing interrogation and bore the marks of beatings. Nearly as distressing were the curses and insults that passed between police and prisoners. Still, Juan maintained his composure, confident that the police were not going to beat or curse him, since he knew nothing about terrorism. Reading the Bible he brought with him to DINCOTE also helped.

Juan's composure shattered around 2.00 a.m. on 21 July when officers pulled him from the cell, threw a hood over his head and dragged him up two flights of stairs, kicking, cursing and insulting him on the way. Juan realized they were taking him to interrogation. 'So, tell us about the map,' they said, once they had arrived. 'You drew it, didn't you?'

'I'm sorry, I don't know what you are talking about, officer.'

Heavy blows to the torso sent streaks of pain through his body. One blow fractured a rib. Still, Juan insisted he knew nothing about a map.

'You're telling us you had nothing to do with Cieneguilla?' the interrogators snapped.

Cieneguilla? Juan recalled having read about that in the papers. It was a garbage dump on the outskirts of Lima where news reporters and human rights investigators had unearthed the remains of several human bodies. 'You know who killed those people, don't you,' the police were saying. 'Maybe you killed them yourself.'

'No, sir. I know nothing . . .'

More blows. His interrogators tore the hood off Juan's head and thrust a paper at him. He saw a hand-drawn map with writing on it. 'Look, Mallea, this is your handwriting, isn't it? Just say it is. Remember, we know where you live. You wouldn't want anything to happen to your wife and that baby boy of yours, would you?'

Juan's stomach tightened into a knot. He swallowed hard. 'Sir, please understand, I am a Christian. I have never had any- thing to do with terrorists or criminals.'

His answer infuriated the interrogators. A fist smashed into his jaw, breaking a tooth. More blows, more cursing and insults. Worst of all, more threats against Cristina and Juancito. The interrogators kept at their work most of the night. To the end, Juan Mallea insisted he knew nothing about terrorism nor the map of Cieneguilla.

*   *   *

The events that culminated in the detention and torture of Juan Mallea originated at the Cantuta National University one year previously. On a July afternoon in 1992, the university convened a meeting of students at the behest of the security forces. The authorities wanted to discuss several pressing issues with people at Cantuta, including a car bomb that had exploded in the posh Lima district of Miraflores. The meeting, tense at the outset, degenerated into a shouting match. One student, a Ms Vertila Lozano, insulted a military officer, a certain Lieutenant Medina. According to witnesses, Ms Lozano called Lt Medina a 'wretched dog'. At that point, a faculty member, a certain Professor Muñoz, intervened and called for calm. The security officers withdrew from the meeting. According to witnesses, Lt Medina threatened Ms Lozano as he was leaving. 'We will be back for you,' he said.

That same night, hooded gunmen stole onto the Cantuta National University campus, entered a dormitory and abducted nine students from their rooms. Ms Lozano was one of them. She was never seen alive again. Professor Muñoz disappeared from campus the same night, as well. No one knew the fate of the missing until mid-1993, when a Lima journalist came into possession of a hand-drawn map of the Cieneguilla garbage dump. The map led investigators to a burial site containing charred human remains. Forensic experts identified them as those of the nine students and one professor from Cantuta National University.

The discovery, duly reported in the Peruvian press, embarrassed the security forces. An angry public accused anti-terrorist police of committing a terrorist act themselves. The outcry embarrassed the Peruvian government, as well. Politicians endured harsh criticism for condoning crimes committed against civilians at a time when they stringently punished those who committed crimes against the state. The outcry reached a crescendo when informed sources within the armed forces accused an anti-terrorist 'annihilation team', known as the Colina Group, of committing the Cantuta murders. The authorities knew they must act, and quickly. Thus, on 22 July 1993, Juan Mallea appeared in a nationally broadcast TV news conference. He wore the striped prison uniform of a convicted terrorist and the countenance of a man profoundly confused. He bore the marks of a beating and he stood accused of homicide and treason. Juan Mallea, police investigators declared, had drawn that map of the Cieneguilla garbage dump, where he and his Shining Path accomplices burned and buried the bodies of the Cantuta University students after brutally murdering them.

*   *   *

Mrs Maria Cristina Mallea first learned that her husband stood accused of terrorism when she saw him in the pin-striped prison uniform on television. After absorbing the initial shock, Cristina pondered what to do. She could ill afford a private attorney. It would have done little good to hire one anyway, due to strict anti-terrorist laws that had gone into effect in Peru just before Juan's arrest and which severely restricted the rights of the accused to defend themselves against treason charges. Cristina Mallea did what she thought best. She called Walter Agurto, the pastor of the Christian and Missionary Alliance Church in Comas that she and Juan attended. It was the best thing she could have done. Agurto immediately composed a letter to the National Council of Evangelicals of Peru, CONEP, requesting its help in defending Juan Mallea. CONEP passed the letter along to its human rights department, now known officially as the Peace and Hope Directorate for Social Action and Advancement. Peace and Hope chairman Caleb Meza was out of town at the time, so Agurto's letter reached his assistant, Alfonso Wieland. Wieland alerted the rest of the Peace and Hope staff, which now included Rolando Pérez, a journalist, human rights attorney Germán Vargas and José Regalado's wife, Ruth. They met with Cristina Mallea and Walter Agurto to discuss what they could do. Afterwards, Wieland asked José Regalado to interview Juan Mallea in jail.

> I made contact directly with Juan in an underground cell. I took a small tape recorder with me, managed to get it past security and recorded his testimony. Juan was a bit nervous. Actually, as his legal counsel, I had to be hard on him with the questions and possible accusations he would face. I made him see that even though he was innocent, this was going to be a terrifically difficult case. The church could not play with this thing, it was too sensitive. I even caused him a few tears because he thought we doubted his innocence. Up until then, all we had was hearsay. But after interviewing him, I knew I was dealing with an innocent man.
>
> This was a tense case, totally manipulated by politicians, from the president of the Republic down to the police officers investigating the crime. Military people were telling the press that members of the Colina Group were clearly responsible and described how they did it. The government took advantage of Juan Mallea's arrest to counteract their allegations. They put in his hands a map, which he allegedly drew, in order to incriminate Shining Path. They didn't care who they used. They thought Juan was a nobody and that, if they accused him, no one would stand up for him.
>
> After that first visit with Juan, people began threatening me. 'Juan is a terrorist for sure,' they said. 'If you stick your nose in here, something might happen to your family.' Later, people called on the phone insisting that I drop the case. 'Your life could be in danger. We know who all of you are.' My wife Ruth and I were concerned about this situation, so we submitted it to prayer. We decided the only right thing we could do was to go ahead.

The staff at Peace and Hope were acquainted with pressure, having faced it before in their work defending human rights. Now the pressure increased. Strangers conspicuously loitered outside CONEP offices and tailed staff cars around town. Peace and Hope had learned the best way to deal with such pressure was to apply pressure of its own. Rolando Pérez alerted evangelical churches throughout Peru about the Juan Mallea case and asked them to organize prayer vigils on his behalf. The journalist also fed information from the defence investigation to friends in the news media. Within days, the facts about the plot to incriminate an innocent man for the Cantuta murders appeared in TV documentaries and press reports across Peru. Upon his return to Lima, Caleb Meza alerted a network of international organizations composed of Tearfund, Christian Solidarity International and Open Doors, and asked them to help. Soon Peruvian politicians began receiving letters from concerned Christians in England, Switzerland, Canada, the United States and elsewhere, asking them to ensure that Juan Mallea receive a fair trial.

The pressure produced measurable results. In the short term, the publicity and letters convinced Peruvian politicians that Juan Mallea was somebody who mattered to people and not a nobody whom they could manipulate. In the long term, the pressure ensured that Juan would get a fair trial. In the meantime, many people would invest much work, worry and prayer – especially prayer – in the case of Juan Mallea.

*   *   *

No one invested more in Juan's case than Mrs Cristina Mallea. 'Normally, my wife is quite an easy-going person,' Juan later told a journalist. 'But when they put me in prison, she fought like a lioness for my freedom.'

A school teacher by vocation, Cristina devoted all her spare time to her husband's defence. The work involved collecting documents, meeting officials, paying fees, making phone calls, visiting Juan in jail, meeting more officials, paying more fees. Family and friends cautioned her to ease off, fearing that the frenetic schedule would provoke a miscarriage. 'Don't worry,' she told them, 'I have no doubt this baby will be born. We have letters from brothers all over the world saying that they are praying for Juan, me and the little one.'

Juan agonized over the difficulties his plight imposed on Cristina, to the point that he did not tell her of the difficulties he himself endured behind bars. For instance, jailers provided only two meals a day to inmates, a breakfast of bread and tea and a lunch of soup. The meagre fare barely kept inmates alive. Unless family or friends brought them food from home, prisoners suffered nagging hunger. Juan preferred to endure the hunger rather than to burden his wife with yet another worry. Several weeks into his imprisonment, however, Cristina noticed visitors bringing food to the jail and asked Juan why. He admitted the reason. From then on, Cristina saw to it that her husband ate his favourite meals every day.

Most of Cristina's difficulties had to do with money. Juan's imprisonment obliged her to spend a good deal of it on documents and fees, and since Juan was no longer earning an income, Cristina had less money to spend than usual. One day, four months after Juan's arrest and three days before Cristina's next paycheck, a pickpocket in a court house elevator stole her last bit of cash. The loss devastated her. She knew Juan's parents would gladly feed her and Juancito until payday, but she was ashamed to ask them. That afternoon, a young woman from the United Bible Society dropped by the modest apartment with a thick envelope. A weary Cristina absently slipped it into her pocket, thinking it contained more letters from overseas that she could read later. 'Pardon me, Mrs Mallea,' the young woman said, 'I think you will want to look in there right away.' Cristina reached into the envelope and pulled out a bundle of US dollars. The timing stunned her. 'It was as if God himself sent it,' she later told her husband on a visit to the jail. 'I did not have a cent left in the house.'

When Juan was transferred to the Castro Castro maximum security prison, visits from Cristina decreased dramatically – to exactly one, 30-minute visit each month, as prescribed by Peru's strict anti-terrorist laws. Castro Castro inmates could not receive phone calls either, so these visits were the only communication between the couple. Despite her progressing pregnancy, Cristina did not miss a visit, until December. That month, Juan's father appeared on the appointed day to tell him that Cristina was not coming because, hours before, her doctor had admitted her to hospital due to an unexpected complication with the pregnancy. That was all Juan's father knew at the time. For 12 days, Juan worried about the fate of his wife and their unborn child. He would have worried 30 days, except that Castro Castro granted inmates an extra visitors' day in December, in honour of Christmas. To his great relief, Cristina appeared on the appointed day carrying little Caleb, their new baby boy named for Caleb Meza of Peace and Hope. Juan stared in wonder, aching to hold his loved ones in his arms. But anti-terrorist law dictated that prison visits take place through a thick partition. That day, however, the law was broken. Juan heard the gruff voice of the duty officer: 'Let this woman and her child come through.' He thought his ears had deceived him, but suddenly there stood Cristina and tiny Caleb before him. For a few precious minutes, the three Malleas stood together in close embrace. It was, of course, the first time Juan had held Caleb in his arms. It was also the first time, since the day the strangers took him from their modest apartment, that he had held Cristina in his arms.

That gruff voice belonged to a certain Lieutenant Eguiluz. The duty officer had taken an interest in Juan Mallea and his case.

Lieutenant Eguiluz helped me, at great risk to himself. Against prison rules, he brought me things so that I could do hand crafts. I made baskets, dolls, rugs and so forth. The work was therapeutic. In Castro Castro, they gave us one half-hour of exercise per day. The other twenty-three and a half hours we spent in the cell. The worst part of being in prison is doing nothing all day.

I had lots of time to reflect on things, not so much worrying about myself as for the people in the prison from faraway, who lived in the mountains and other parts of the interior. They were in a much worse predicament than I. I started sharing the Word and, almost immediately they started asking questions. A lot of people wanted to hear the Word of God. I succeeded in identifying a brother here, another there. We were able to organize a Bible hour. We would stand at the door of our cells and shout, 'Bible Hour starts now!' We'd read loudly from the Bible so that everybody could hear. We started with a small group of three or four. Later about 30 per cent of the cell block was participating every day.

*   *   *

Peace and Hope faced a tough legal battle in order to free Juan Mallea from jail. To lead the defence team, Caleb Meza contracted José Pablo Mora, a veteran human rights attorney, to work alongside Peace and Hope lawyers Germán Vargas, Alfonso Wieland and José and Ruth Regalado. The defence team knew it must accomplish two daunting legal feats to get Juan Mallea out of jail.

The first was to refute the police's claim that Juan had drawn the map of the Cieneguilla garbage dump. Police officials had produced expert testimony from a graphotechnologist which asserted that the map bore handwriting identical to that of Juan Mallea. Peace and Hope quietly collected expert testimony from three more graphotechnologists, each working independently, who asserted that the handwriting on the Cieneguilla map bore no resemblance whatsoever to that of Juan Mallea. When defence lawyers presented the findings to the judge, he ruled that the police evidence was incorrect. First feat accomplished.

Success did not come without its price. Donations from Tearfund and other concerned Christian organizations allowed Peace and Hope to meet legal expenses, such as lawyers' salaries and graphotechnologist fees. Yet, defending Juan Mallea cost more than just money.

'A document surfaced in the Ministry of the Interior accusing me of being a "terrorist attorney",' José Regalado later told a journalist. 'The document was of a confidential nature, probably circulated by the Intelligence Service. It mentioned me by name as a lawyer who defended Shining Path. That meant they had placed me under surveillance. They could have arrested me at any moment and accused me of working for Shining Path.'

Once again, Peace and Hope met pressure with pressure of its own. They informed the Lima Bar Association of the confidential report. The Bar Association appealed to the Inter-American Court. Soon, the Supreme Court of Peru was aware that the Intelligence Service had placed José Regalado under surveillance. The judge hearing the case issued a restraining order that guaranteed José's personal security. The surveillance ceased.

The second feat the defence team had to accomplish took staggering persistence. Yet to fail in it would seal Juan Mallea's fate. Peace and Hope lawyers had to convince the court to drop the charge of treason. Under Peru's strict anti-terrorist laws, treason cases were tried before a military tribunal of 'faceless' judges. The magistrates actually wore hoods to conceal their identity. Faceless judges were licensed to convict defendants on the slimmest of evidence and sentence them to long years in prison. Treason carried a minimum sentence of 20 years, maximum penalty – life. The verdicts of military tribunals could not be overturned by civil courts. Should Juan face a panel of faceless judges, he would likely never again hold Cristina, Juancito or tiny Caleb in his arms.

Prosecutors for the state argued that Juan Mallea was a Shining Path terrorist and should be tried as such. Defence attorney José Mora and his team argued that the state had failed to produce convincing evidence linking Juan to the Path. The only material evidence, in fact, was the map of Cieneguilla, which had proved to be a forgery. Therefore, Mora argued, a civil court had jurisdiction over Juan Mallea, not the military. After long months of arguments, the case came before the Supreme Court of Peru, which ruled that, due to lack of any compelling evidence, the treason charge against Juan Mallea be dismissed. He was free to go.

On 27 April 1994, nearly ten months after his arrest, Juan Mallea walked out of Castro Castro prison. Following an emotional reunion, Peace and Hope arranged for the Mallea family to spend several months in Chile recuperating from their ordeal. Upon his return to Peru, Juan resumed the life he had led before his imprisonment. At least it appeared so. But inwardly he was a changed man.

'God has taught me a great many objective lessons for life,' he told a friend. 'I found that two things predominate in jail:

tuberculosis and insanity. I've had the opportunity to experience compelling truth and I believe God now expects something extra of me.'

*   *   *

The entire Christian community in Peru, as well as many Christians abroad, celebrated Juan Mallea's acquittal. Once his innocence was established, justice proceeded in the Cantuta case. The real murderers were apprehended, tried and convicted. This was but one outcome of the Mallea case. The publicity it generated drew attention to the plight of hundreds of other innocent Peruvians behind bars, falsely accused of involvement with Shining Path. Most of them were, like Juan Mallea, 'nobodies' whose only crime was to be in the wrong place at the wrong time. Furthermore, statistics gathered by the staff of Peace and Hope showed that some 150 of the innocent prisoners were, like Juan Mallea, evangelical Christians.

Alfonso Wieland succeeded Caleb Meza as director of Peace and Hope in January 1994. Wieland, trained in sociology and law, set about analysing the information human rights workers had gathered on the imprisoned. He found that some were as young as 16, others were grandparents. Many were illiterate peasants from the mountains who understood nothing of their alleged crime. None, Wieland found, deserved to spend 20 years to life behind bars.

So why were they there? Most were imprisoned under Peru's strict anti-terrorist laws, decreed by President Alberto Fujimori in 1992. Many of the cases involved the controversial 'repented terrorist' clause, which reduced prison sentences for *senderistas* who provided police with the names of their accomplices. The new laws also endowed law enforcement officials with extraordinary powers. Police could detain a suspect up to 30 days, denying him visits from family and lawyers, and not even inform him of the reason for his arrest. Incentives for arresting suspected terrorists abounded. Ambitious police officers could gain rapid promotion up the ranks for pulling in such suspects. Corrupt police officers could demand payment of an 'investigative quota' from the suspects they arrested.

Prices ranged from $500 to $2,000 dollars, depending on the seriousness of the allegations. Police routinely dropped charges against prisoners who paid the quota. Prisoners unwilling or unable to pay were doomed. The new laws failed to hold the police accountable for such corruption. In fact, they granted the security forces virtual impunity. The officers who attempted to blackmail Juan Mallea, for example, received only a feeble citation scolding them for 'judicial errors' committed during their investigation of the Cantuta murders.

The Shining Path war had produced yet another appalling tragedy for Peru. Terrorism had conspired with the law to put innocent teenagers, grandparents, housewives, auto mechanics, farmers, teachers and students behind bars for 20 years to life.

'As the saying goes,' Alfonso Wieland told a visiting journalist, 'the righteous pay the price for the sinners.'

*   *   *

Until 20 November 1992, Mrs Antonia Jaimes worked as a fish merchant in Lima's Israelitas Market. A diminutive woman with a shy smile and glossy black hair gathered in a tight bun, Antonia sits at a table in the Peace and Hope office and recalls the night she and her husband were accused of building a car bomb for the Path.

I was at home at 12 o'clock midnight when they knocked on the gate that opens to the street. I answered the knock and they said they were policemen. They wanted me to open the gate.

'This gate does not open, it's sealed shut,' I said. 'I will have to open the small door for you.'

When I did, several armed officers rushed inside. They said, 'What is your name?'

'Mrs Antonia Alfaro Jaimes.'

'Your papers, please.'

I handed them over and they said, 'Who do you live with?'

'With my husband and four children.'

'No one else lives in the house?'

'No one else. Who else would be living here?'

They asked my husband for his documents. Then they said, 'A car bomb came from this house.'

I said, 'What is a car bomb? I don't know what that is.'

'Don't start that,' they replied. 'Turn on the lights.'

'I don't have electricity, sir. But if you want, I can light a candle.'

I lit the candle and they began searching the whole house. When they finished, even though they had found nothing, they said, 'You are coming with us.'

I said, 'Fine, sir, I'm not afraid. I am going to clear up this whole matter.'

As I was leaving, the police captain said to me, 'This house will be shut up. They are going to give you life imprisonment.'

'But sir, I had nothing to do with this thing,' I said. 'You can see for yourself that an automobile could not possibly pass through our gate, it has been sealed shut for years. Are they going to give me life imprisonment without any proof?'

'Find somebody to look after your kids,' he said. They took us away.

At that time, my youngest daughter was two and a half years old. I left her weeping.

9

Return to Huamanga

Ayacucho, September 1992

Nearly three years passed before Rómulo Sauñe could visit his grandfather's grave in Chakiqpampa. Danger was only part of the reason. With the publication of the *Ayacucho Bible*, Rómulo had gained international notoriety. Invitations to speak came from places as diverse as Mexico, Alaska and Israel. Rómulo served as a Quecha translator for Billy Graham in the evangelist's Buenos Aires crusade. Campus Crusade for Christ recruited him to record the voice of Christ on the Quechua sound-track of the well-known *Jesus* film. The World Evangelical Fellowship summoned Rómulo to Manila, Philippines, and granted him its first Religious Freedom Award for 'consistent and courageous efforts to proclaim and maintain a witness of Jesus Christ amidst harsh repression and terrorism'.

In 1992, the Sauñes settled into a temporary home in Atlanta, Georgia, near Donna's parents. They had scheduled a year-long furlough for rest and reunions with Donna's family, who had returned to the States from missionary service in New Guinea. As often happens with missionary families, however, things did not happen as planned. In August, Rómulo made a trip to Quito, Ecuador, for an international evangelism conference. He decided to use the opportunity to go on to Peru and pay his respects in Chakiqpampa.

In the first days of September, Rómulo arrived in the village with both his parents, his brother Ruben, his uncle Arcangel Quicaña; his 21-year-old nephew, Marco Antonio, his cousin Josué, the son of Antonia Quicaña; and two godchildren, Alfredo and Margarita Fajardo. He needed plenty of help to prepare the *pachamanca*, a traditional Inca banquet he would serve the village as a tribute to his dead grandfather. Joshua Sauñe had also planned to attend the commemoration in Chakiqpampa. But Rómulo telephoned him on the eve of Joshua's departure from Arizona, saying it would be best if he stayed at home.

That puzzling phone call turned out to be but the first of several odd incidents that occurred during the visit. On his international travels, Rómulo had collected special gifts for his neighbours and a bouquet of silk flowers for Justiniano's grave. But to his dismay, the things went missing when he reached Chakiqpampa. The Sauñes went door to door, delivering personal invitations to the *pachamanca* to every family in the village. However, few of their neighbours came to partake of the feast. The snub depressed the usually cheerful Rómulo. 'I wanted everybody to come, since this will be my last day here,' he remarked to his father. Enrique would remember those words as a portent.

That night, Rómulo and Ruben slept fitfully in the loft of a neighbour's adobe house. Their muffled cries awoke Enrique, sleeping below. He asked his sons about their nightmares next morning, but they declined to share the content of the dreams. Their mother Zoila had been nervous about this whole Chakiqpampa venture and they did not want to agitate her. An uneasy gloom hung over the family as they hiked the two hours out to the road. Teofila Quicaña accompanied them as far as Paccha and stood watching as they drove off in Arcangel's jeep. She overheard a woman murmur: 'What a pity. Which of the poor people in that white jeep will die today?' Teofila would remember those words as a portent.

The Path, which boasted 'a thousand eyes and a thousand ears' had the Sauñe family under surveillance. *Senderistas* knew what time the Sauñes stopped for lunch at a roadside restaurant on the way home and when the family left the restaurant to continue their journey. The Path knew when the white jeep would reach the ambush they had prepared. They even knew which of the passengers were to die that day.

The Path had set up the ambush on a blind curve above the

city of Ayacucho. It was a well-concealed spot that the terrorists had used before to waylay travellers. The Sauñes could not see the roadblock, nor the 500 terrorists spread out on the mountain slope above, until they had fallen into the trap. The *senderistas* had already detained a dozen other vehicles and were taking money, food and valuables from the passengers. Enrique watched the terrorists prepare to set fire to a bus, a symbolic act that demonstrated their disdain for the government. The driver argued with the terrorists, attempting to save the vehicle. He lost the quarrel. Enrique saw the flash of a machete and the man's head topple from his shoulders.

A terrorist pointed his gun at Arcangel.'Pull this automobile to the other side of the road,' he ordered.'All of you men step out and form a line against that embankment.'

The five Quicaña–Sauñe men lined up side by side and the *senderistas* checked their identification papers.'You there, step out of the line,' a terrorist said to Enrique. Mr Sauñe did not move. He intended to die with his sons. The terrorists pulled him from the line. Enrique returned to his place.'I said to get out of the way!' the *senderista* barked, shoving Enrique to the side. He returned to his place. The terrorist shrugged and cocked his weapon. That instant, the firing commenced. Zoila grabbed Enrique by the arm and pulled him away from the hail of bullets.

Ruben was the first to fall, then Josué, then Arcangel and Marco Antonio. Rómulo, at the far end of the line, looked fondly at his parents as bullets tore into his chest. He drew a last, deep breath and fell dead.

'Lord have mercy,' Zoila said. She and Enrique stood silent as the *senderistas* removed shoes, clothing and valuables from their sons' bodies. The Sauñes did not weep for their loved ones in that moment. Shock was only part of the reason. Descendants of the Inca do not permit enemies to see their tears.

*   *   *

All during the long journey from Arizona to Ayacucho, Joshua Sauñe did not weep either. He still could not believe the news he had received from his sister-in-law, Donna, when she called from Atlanta that Sunday morning. 'Your brothers were killed yesterday,' she said. That simply could not be true. Joshua had to go to see for himself that this thing had happened. Until then, he could not weep.

He could be angry, however. Joshua was very angry. He was angry with the Path for killing Ruben, Rómulo and his cousins and he was angry with God for letting it happen. 'Where were your angels when those people were slaughtering my brothers?' he asked bitterly. 'Maybe they were cowards, hiding behind the mountain.' Joshua was no coward. He knew exactly what he would do when he arrived in Ayacucho. He would find Carlos Trisollini. The two of them would find guns and together they would go and kill the people who killed his brothers. According to the blood pact they had made as boys, now that Ruben was dead, it fell to Joshua and Carlos to avenge him.

All during the long journey from Arizona to Ayacucho, Joshua plotted revenge. Of course, he would kill the *senderistas* who had ambushed his family. But he knew of others who helped commit the crime. A *chanka* who had business dealings with the family betrayed his brothers. 'Those miserable Sauñes are the ones who brought the Yankee imperialists here to evangelize us,' the man told the Path. 'Rómulo has been all around the world, has lots of foreigners for friends. Why, the Sauñe boys are even married to foreigners.' The *chanka* must have felt a slight twinge of conscience, however. 'One thing,' he added, 'please, don't do anything to the father, okay?'

Joshua felt no twinge of conscience. He intended to kill first the grandparents and parents of his brothers' murderers, then their sisters, brothers, spouses and children, before killing the murderers themselves.

As expected, Carlos Trisollini was waiting for Joshua at the Ayacucho airport. Their eyes met across the crowded terminal and Joshua knew that Carlos had everything ready. As soon as he collected his bags and got through the door, they would be off to do the deed.

Getting out of the door was the problem, for there stood Zoila Sauñe awaiting her son. It surprised Joshua to see his mother at the airport. He assumed she would be home resting, half-dead with grief. But there she stood, calm, composed and colourfully dressed in her best Quechua clothes. She took her son firmly by the arm and guided him towards a waiting taxi.

'Joshua, I know what you're thinking,' Zoila said, 'but it's not worth it. Better you come with me to where your brothers are lying at the church.' Before he realized what was happening, Joshua found himself squeezed into the back seat of the taxi between his mother and his uncle Arcangel. There was no way he could get to Carlos now.

On the way to his brothers' funeral, Joshua heard the account of how his uncle had survived the *senderista* firing squad. When the shooting started, Arcangel was knocked to the ground – whether by a passing bullet or a falling body, he could not tell. As he lay there in shock, a *senderista* walked up and discovered he was still alive. The terrorist pointed his weapon at Arcangel's chest and pulled the trigger, but the gun did not fire. It was empty. Before he could reload, the beating of an approaching army helicopter sent him and his comrades fleeing up the mountain slope. The gunship opened fire, cutting down two dozen of the terrorists, including some of those who had murdered the Quicaña–Sauñe men just moments before. Ground troops sent from Ayacucho followed up the attack and chased the Path over the mountain ridge, killing more terrorists. Although he was thankful to see his uncle alive, Joshua could not help but wonder why that army helicopter had not arrived in time to save the rest of his family.

Mourners packed the Presbyterian church where the funeral was about to begin. A journalist estimated that a crowd of between 4,000 and 5,000 turned out to grieve the four Quicaña–Sauñe men, by far the largest funeral held in Ayacucho in years. Before Joshua realized what was happening, he was at the front of the church looking down on the caskets of his dead brothers. His father stood beside him. 'Joshua, you are the only son I have here. You must speak on behalf of your brothers.'

Joshua had not expected to say anything at the funeral. Indeed, he had not even expected to attend the funeral. Yet, as he looked around at the faces of grieving Quechuas, he immediately knew what he would say when he stood before them. 'Shining Path has been killing us long enough! Join me, my brothers, and we will rise up and fight them. It is time for revenge!'

At that moment, a tearful Carlos Trisollini came and embraced him. 'Joshua, you are not crying,' Carlos said. 'Why don't you cry?'

'I can't cry just yet,' Joshua answered. Then he told his old friend the truth. 'I'm too angry to cry, Carlos.'

It was time for Joshua to enter the Presbyterian pulpit. The mourners recognized him and fell silent. They noticed that the unruly youth who left Peru a decade ago had matured into a dignified man. The man bore a striking resemblance to his Inca ancestors: square, muscular physique; steady, coal-black eyes and measured baritone voice.

'My brothers and sisters,' Joshua said, 'we are not fighting against flesh and blood, but against principalities and powers in heavenly places.'

Joshua blinked. He had not planned to say that. He did not even remember having read the verse, Ephesians 3.10, in the Bible, nor could he recall how the words got into his head. Nevertheless, that is what he said.

'Shining Path is not my enemy,' he continued. 'Satan is my enemy. We are actually fighting against the devil, not the people who killed my brothers. They need Christ just as you and I do.'

Before he realized what was happening, God had changed Joshua Sauñe's heart. 'I suddenly saw the people who killed my brother as my people also,' he later told a friend. 'If I was going to fight Shining Path, I should fight with the Bible. It was the first time I understood that. I, a man who grew up thinking that he would change his people by fighting.'

After the worship service, Joshua and Carlos helped carry the caskets of Rómulo, Ruben, Josué and Marco Antonio to the Ayacucho cemetery, leading the funeral procession. Most of the 5,000 mourners were colourfully dressed Quechuas, some of whom had walked for days from the mountains and jungles to pay their last respects to the martyrs. All who attended the funeral were putting themselves at risk. Shining Path infiltrators were there, noting who came to mourn these enemies of the revolution. The next funerals in Ayacucho might be for the mourners themselves.

That evening, Carlos Trisollini brought several friends to the Plaza Hotel where Joshua was staying. 'Okay, the funeral is over, now let's go,' he said to Joshua. 'I know where the *senderistas* are headed. They're going towards the jungle.'

Joshua sighed. 'Carlos, when I came from the United States, I wanted to kill,' he said. 'That's what I felt in my heart. But after seeing the funeral and the truth of what happened, I don't want to do that any more.'

'But, Joshua, remember our promise! We have to avenge Ruben. Everything is ready. We have to go now.'

'Carlos, I don't think we're going to change our people that way. God has changed my heart. I know now He has something more for me.'

'Joshua, even if you don't go, I must go.'

'We have different ways of doing things, you and I,' Joshua said. 'This is my way of doing it. I don't want my children to hate. Hating not just Shining Path, but hating white people, hating the Spanish for what they did to us. I don't want that any more.

'The hate is going to stop with me,' he concluded. 'I'm not going to pass it on to my children. I will return to the States, and when I come back, it will be with different ways of fighting this thing that is happening here.'

Carlos insisted no more. The two friends prayed together, then said good night. The next day Joshua left Ayacucho for the USA. He would not try to punish the Path for the deaths of his loved ones. Nevertheless punishment was coming, and swiftly.

* * *

The *senderistas* who killed the Quicaña–Sauñe men had gathered from terrorist bases in Ica, Cachi, Huancavelica and the lower Apurimac basin. When the army counter-attacked that

Saturday, some 100 guerrillas fell in the fighting. The rest retreated towards their home bases. Few made it. The next morning, army troops intercepted one column crossing the ridge of Huaytará and eliminated all 40 of the *senderistas*.

Civil defence forces mobilized when news of the killings reached the villages of rural Huamanga. On a path below Socos, one patrol encountered a band of strangers whom they suspected of being members of Shining Path. 'Where is our brother Rómulo?' the patrol asked them. 'What have you done to him?' In reply, the strangers pulled out weapons. A gunfight ensued. When it ended, the strangers all lay dead.

The largest contingent of *senderistas* made a forced march towards the jungles of the lower Apurimac, trying to escape pursuing army troops. En route, the terrorists were unable to find anyone willing to feed them and grew weak from hunger and fatigue. One guerrilla was heard to complain to a comrade. 'Those men must have been innocent. Why did we kill them? We wouldn't be suffering like this if we had not done so.'

The army caught up with the guerrillas before they could reach sanctuary in the jungle. Trapped in a canyon and too exhausted to put up a fight, the *senderistas* fell before a punishing barrage of gunfire. The army destroyed the entire column, some 300 guerrillas. Soldiers then despoiled the dead terrorists of items stolen from their victims, including the clothing they had taken from the Quicaña–Sauñe men. In fact, the Path suffered such slaughter that day that virtually none was left to punish the mourners who had attended the four martyrs' funeral.

On Saturday, 12 September 1992, exactly one week after the Quicaña–Sauñe men were killed, anti-terrorist police stormed a Lima apartment they had been keeping under surveillance. Inside they found Abimael Guzman Reynosa and several key members of the Shining Path high command. As officers cuffed him to take him into custody, the haughty Presidente Gonzalo said, 'This time, it's my turn to lose.'

Guzman lost in a big way. Television networks broadcast press conferences with the fallen Shining Path leader. The authorities felt it was time to introduce the public to the shadowy figure who had terrorized Peru for more than a decade. Presidente Gonzalo went on the air, answering reporters' questions from behind the bars of a prison cage. His performance was a public relations disaster for the Path. The image of a heroic freedom fighter, which Guzman had carefully cultivated while in hiding, dissolved once Peruvians saw the man for what he really was: a chubby, middle-aged academic who chain-smoked imported cigarettes while ranting about his plan to liberate the poor.

Young rebels suffered acute disillusionment when they beheld, with their own eyes, the real Presidente Gonzalo. The terrorist movement that Guzman had managed so shrewdly began to unravel, as recruits abandoned the Path by the hundreds. In fact, disillusionment hurt the Path as much as the costly military defeats they suffered in the latter months of 1992. Within two years, the once feared Shining Path virtually self-destructed. It was one of the most dramatic reversals in any civil war of the twentieth century.

Should you ask Peruvians how and why this happened, you will hear various explanations. Some say a change in military strategy defeated the Path, others credit the civilian militias. A few experts, such as noted anthropologist Carlos Ivan Degregori, say that evangelical Christians' resistance to Marxist–Leninist–Maoist doctrine was a key factor. And of course, there were the prayers.

Should you ask 70-year-old Enrique Sauñe why the Path failed, he will tell you that it was because God answered those prayers, even at great cost to himself and his family.

'God had a plan, a remedy prepared for the pacification of the country,' he told a visiting journalist. 'It began with my sons.'

*   *   *

Although Missy Sauñe and her husband customarily did most of their talking in the car, they did not talk much on the way home from the airport. The long flight back to Arizona from Ayacucho was still not enough time for Joshua to get used to the fact that his brothers were gone. Missy knew Joshua was not ready to talk just yet and she would wait until he was. Missy waited three months.

The couple were taking a day trip in their car when Joshua finally talked about his brothers. He said: 'I think I need to go to Peru and take over their ministry. There's no one else. I have to do it.'

Missy had been expecting Joshua to say something like this since before she married him. She had her answer ready. 'Okay.'

Missy Aspa met Joshua Sauñe in 1987, when she was finishing high school and he was studying art in Phoenix. One Sunday, Joshua and his brother Abel visited the Poston, Arizona, Baptist Church on the Colorado River Indian Reservation. That is where the Aspa family, native Comanches, made their home. In June 1988, Joshua married Missy in the Poston Baptist Church and the couple settled in the nearby town of Parker. Joshua launched his art career and Missy went to work in an office. Joshua's career prospered. The Thunderbird Art Association began marketing his native American jewellery and sculptures of hardwood and alabaster. His work sold in galleries and exhibits across the southwestern United States. It seemed the Sauñes would settle permanently in Arizona. Then Joshua went to Ayacucho to bury his brothers.

Since Rómulo's and Ruben's funeral, he had thought long and hard about what their deaths meant in terms of his duty before God to labour for justice among the Quechuas of Huamanga. Joshua could not escape that duty. He had been born, christened even, to perform it.

Missy had only one doubt about Joshua's proposal. 'Do you think that we have enough training to do that?' she asked. 'You know, we've never worked in anything like ministry or missionary service.'

Joshua's answer was to move Missy and their two small children to Phoenix, where the Christian Hope Indian Eskimo Fellowship, a mission organization commonly known as CHIEF, conducted discipleship training. Joshua took classes at the CHIEF mission centre while continuing his art career part-time. Missy completed a nursing degree and took a position as medical assistant in a family health-care centre. The couple lived on the salary she earned and saved the income from Joshua's artwork. They would need those savings one day to move to South America.

Two and a half years after their move to Phoenix, Joshua decided that day had come. He closed his studio and resigned from the Thunderbird Art Association. The President of Thunderbird reacted to the move in a manner typical of the Sauñes' close friends and associates. 'You're going *where*? You're going to do *what*?'

Joshua did not have a precise answer to that second question just yet. His plans for financing a missionary career were fairly vague, as well. CHIEF had recently sent other missionaries overseas, so Joshua and Missy asked the organization to help them formulate a budget and raise support. CHIEF personnel estimated that the Sauñes would need $3,500 dollars a month to cover travel, shipping, visas, equipment, insurance, education, household and office expenses, salary and other outlays. They appealed to supporters and donations for the Sauñes began to arrive at the CHIEF office. However, the donations arrived too slowly to suit Joshua. 'People down in Peru are waiting for us, they're asking when we're coming,' he told Missy. Soon afterwards, the community church the Sauñes attended pledged to support them with $500 dollars per month for one year. With that news, Joshua could wait no longer. In July 1995, he took his savings out of the bank and bought air tickets to Peru.

*   *   *

Joshua and his family settled into the Runa Simi Center in Chosica. Following Rómulo's death, Donna had their house converted into a duplex in order to accommodate Runa Simi co-workers. Now two Sauñe families occupied the quarters. Donna and her four children, Romi, Kusi, Dori and Tawa, on one side; Joshua, Missy, Noconi, Zoyla and Sheyava, on the other. Joshua assumed the position of vice-president of Runa Simi. Over the years, work at the literacy centre had expanded. A sound studio produced recordings of scriptures and hymns in Quechua, as well as other native languages of Peru. Teachers provided specialized training for indigenous Christian pastors and evangelists. Counsellors provided guidance for indigenous families.

Joshua soon expanded the work of Runa Simi further. Two months after arriving in Peru, he and Missy went to Ayacucho to visit the Quechua congregation that Enrique Sauñe pastored in the suburb of Cuchipampa. Cuchipampa, like dozens of refugee neighbourhoods surrounding Ayacucho, contained an astounding number of widows and orphans left in the wake of Shining Path. The sight of so many children roaming the streets, barefoot and underfed, made a strong impression on Joshua. When he looked into their eyes, he saw himself, a poor Quechua child. But a child to whom God gave the opportunity to become an affluent artist.

'May I ask you something?' he said to the children's widowed mothers. 'Are your kids attending school?'

'No,' they answered. 'There is no way for us to send them to school. We cannot afford the fees and our children must work to help support us.'

Apart from the obvious need for an education, other compelling reasons existed for these orphans to attend school. Carlos Trisollini described to Joshua the tragic impact the terrorist war had on these children. Some, at age four or five, witnessed their own fathers murdered by the Path. That trauma was resurfacing now that the kids had reached their teens. They formed gangs in Cuchipampa and other refugee neighbourhoods. The result was as ironic as it was tragic. Quechua children, who years before had escaped Shining Path violence in rural Huamanga, were now dying violently on the streets of Ayacucho.

Missy and Joshua agreed that their first missionary undertaking would be to establish a school in Cuchipampa. Due to limited funds, they began with just ten pupils, but planned to add ten more pupils each year until the school became self-supporting. The following year, the government completed a road from Paccha to Chakiqpampa. The Sauñes saw this as an opportunity to establish a school for orphans there, as well.

They gave the Chakiqpampa establishment the same name as the one in Cuchipampa: The Rómulo Sauñe Primary School.

While working on the school projects, Joshua grew more aware of the acute poverty Shining Path had left in its wake. 'These children are not eating right,' he told Missy one day. 'Most of the time, they eat only barley and water, that's it.'

Joshua got an idea. 'Why don't we purchase land?' he said. 'It could produce all kinds of food for these children.' The idea spawned the Sauñes' second missionary undertaking: the *ayllu huasi*. In Quechua, the term literally means 'clan home' and refers to ancient Inca custom. In the days of the empire, extended families owned and cultivated the land communally, sharing the harvests with neighbours too weak or too old to work. It was the Inca answer to social security.

Joshua and Missy raised money to purchase a tract of land on the Cachi River near Mayubamba for an *ayllu huasi*. Enrique and Zoila Sauñe took charge of planting corn, potatoes and grain on the land and distributing the harvest to widows and orphans, particularly to orphans enrolled in the Rómulo Sauñe Primary Schools. Ultimately, Joshua hoped, they could raise money to build communal homes on the *ayllu huasi*, so that widows could themselves plant and harvest the crops and orphans could learn marketable skills while going to school.

*   *   *

Joshua recruited Alfredo Fajardo to help with these missionary undertakings. Alfredo and his wife Margarita had accompanied Rómulo on his fateful visit to Chakiqpampa. Alfredo would surely have died with Rómulo that day, had his vintage flatbed truck not broken down on the way home. The delay kept the Fajardo family from falling into the fatal ambush. Alfredo concluded that God had spared his life so that he could carry on Rómulo's ministry to the Quechua people.

Alfredo helped Joshua implement yet another of his ideas. At his brothers' funeral, Joshua observed a tangible unity among the massive crowd of Quechua Christians. Though from different clans and denominations, they had come together to mourn the martyrs. He perceived that the terrorist war had produced a profound change of attitude among evangelical Quechuas. They no longer thought of themselves first as Presbyterians or Pentecostals or Assemblies of God, but simply as Christians. Joshua hoped to forge that spirit of unity into cooperative ventures in evangelism and community service.

Alfredo Fajardo and Joshua began criss-crossing the Andes mountains to hold inter-denominational evangelistic campaigns and Bible conferences. One campaign in 1997 took place in San Martin, a small town on the Peruvian *altiplano* near Lake Titicaca. The evangelists pitched a tent next door to the community centre and spent a week showing gospel films and preaching. San Martin residents showed keen interest in the presentations, especially the gospel films. By the last evening of the campaign, Joshua and Alfredo had but one film left in their repertoire. *Trial by Fire* was its name. Produced by the Open Doors organization, the film documented the stories of Christians who have suffered for their faith. Some of the stories were of Peruvian Christians who suffered at the hands of Shining Path.

When Joshua proposed screening the film, Alfredo posed a thoughtful question. 'Do you think this is a good day to die, my brother? You know, there are still *senderistas* around here. Some will be here tonight. If they see this film and decide we are enemies of the revolution, they will try to kill us.'

Joshua pondered this. 'But look at it this way, Alfredo,' he said. 'If they don't kill us, what an opportunity we'll have to lead them to Christ!'

The two evangelists showed *Trial by Fire* that night to a packed tent. When it ended, the crowd sat in uneasy silence, unsure of what would happen next. Joshua stood up and began telling them about the Christ who could sustain his followers through the darkest hours of life. He invited any of them who wanted to meet Christ to make their way to a room in the community centre next door and talk with Alfredo Fajardo and other counsellors who were waiting there. People began filtering out of the tent and headed next door. By the end of the evening, counsellors had prayed with 80 people to receive

Christ. Alfredo suspected, though he did not ask, that some of those who prayed were *senderistas*.

'That night was a highlight of my life,' Joshua later told a friend. 'I, who had once hated the Path so much, saw them come to Christ with my own eyes.'

In 1999, Alfredo Fajardo returned to San Martin without Joshua to hold evangelistic services in the tent. Local residents responded even more favourably than they had two years previously. Some 120 people responded to the invitation to receive Christ. Again, Alfredo suspected, though he did not ask, that several of them were *senderistas*.

Due to the remarkable response to the gospel presentations, Joshua Sauñe assumed that the Shining Path terrorists who once sought to kill him and his family were no longer a threat. In this, he was mistaken.

10

The Battle for Poyeni

When Shining Path attacked in the pre-dawn darkness on that day in May 1990, Tsiriari was still asleep. The Ashaninka village lay on the main road between Mazamari and Puerto Ocopa and considered itself safe from an all-out *senderista* assault. Civil defence commanders had taken the precaution of posting sentinels around the village, but the guards carried only bows and arrows. Those weapons were no match for terrorist machine guns and grenades. Two of the Ashaninka militia, Tito Mahuanca and Juan Peña, fell dead in the hail of bullets. The rest surrendered or fled into the hills.

Pastor Augosto Diaz of the Ashaninka Evangelical Church in Tsiriari and his family were awakened by the gunfire and explosions. As the sun rose, they saw *senderistas* moving into town, tossing dynamite into the homes of their neighbours. Before the Path reached his house, Augosto, his seven children and his wife Mariera, who was seven months pregnant, escaped into the hills. The guerrillas looted the Diaz home of blankets, clothing, tools, pots and pans, then set fire to the cane and palm thatch building. By noon, every material thing Augosto and Mariera owned, except for the clothes on their backs, had been reduced to ashes.

For the next seven months, the Diaz family lived in the hills surrounding Tsiriari, hiding from Shining Path. They lived off what they could glean from the small plots of manioc, corn and plantains Augosto cultivated in the jungle and the fish he could catch in the rivers. They slept under trees or in temporary shelters of palm branches. In July, Mariera gave birth to her eighth child, a boy they named Jagin. The family suffered from hunger, drenching rain and swarming mosquitoes. But they survived. All ten of them, even Jagin.

The months dragged on and the Path remained firmly in control of Tsiriari. Mariera grew more and more despondent. Augosto realized he needed to find a permanent refuge for his family. In December, he was able to reach Mazamari, where fellow pastors of the Ashaninka Evangelical Church were holding an annual training conference. There he spoke with Paul Friesen about his predicament and asked the missionary to help him relocate to one of the Ashaninka refugee towns on the Tambo River. When the pastors conference ended, Augosto and Mariera moved with their children to Betania. The Diaz family would not return home to Tsiriari for five long years.

Augosto, however, did return to the hills near his home from time to time. He went, along with other Ashaninka pastors, to encourage Christian believers still living in the area, teaching them Bible classes and leading prayer meetings. Sometimes, they brought refugees back with them to live in the cramped refugee towns along the Tambo. Pedro Aurelio of Potsoteni, who was then studying in the Bible college at the Swiss Indian Mission near Pucallpa, also made several visits to the Ashaninka living in the areas controlled by Shining Path. Aurelio brought back distressing reports on living conditions there.

'We have seen the grave situation in our community. There are many deaths among our clans; innocent women and children also killed. The terrorists force them to go and fight against the rich and the military. Since the children and elderly cannot defend themselves in these battles, they are killed.

'We have rescued many people who suffered hunger and nakedness under the terrorists' control. They ate leaves to keep from starving. Many of them are sick with anaemia and tuberculosis. For lack of medicines, some are dying.'

Paul and Maurine Friesen did what they could to help Ashaninka families caught in the war between the tribe, the Path and the army. With donated funds from Mennonite Brethren churches in North America and the Mennonite Central Committee, the Friesens purchased basic household goods and temporarily converted their modest home on the campus of the Swiss Indian Mission into a warehouse and shipping centre. Before the war ended, the Friesens would distribute some $30,000 dollars worth of blankets, tools, mosquito nets, clothing, pots and pans to Ashaninka families struggling to survive the Troubles.

'We supplied them with the very basics of living,' Paul Friesen later told a visiting journalist. 'We could send out very little food because the logistics of that would have been overwhelming. We would not have been able to support a lot of people. They had to start raising their own food in the villages where they went.

'I don't know of anyone starving to death or dying because they didn't get enough aid – where aid was available. Now, some places that were under terrorist control, there was no way you could send aid. People there suffered from malnutrition and sickness.'

*   *   *

The first attack on Poyeni came on 14 September 1992. At 6.00 a.m., 200 Shining Path guerrillas opened fire on the town with machine guns, automatic weapons and grenades. Ashaninka defenders, armed with aged rifles, shotguns, bows and arrows, returned the fire. It was not a fair fight. The Ashaninka, ill-prepared for the assault and burdened with the care of hundreds of women and children, faced a disciplined enemy that enjoyed superior firepower. From a military point of view, the fight could not last long. It did not. After three hours, the shooting stopped. Shining Path beat a full-scale retreat.

The battle for Poyeni had begun.

Strategically located on a 500-foot bluff overlooking a bend in the Tambo River, Poyeni commanded a broad view of the surrounding country. It was the type of commanding view that determined the location of fortresses on rivers in medieval Europe. The Ashaninka, in fact, had converted Poyeni into a fortress. Its mission: to block the advance of Shining Path down the Tambo River and so protect Shevoja, Betania, Atalaya, and dozens of other refugee settlements there from attack.

War refugees from Potsoteni, Centro Caperocía and a dozen other villages upriver settled in Poyeni. The town experienced a six-fold increase in population, from 360 to 2,010 residents. The crowding strained local resources to breaking point. Ashaninka farmers could not feed everyone on the limited amount of arable land available to them, no matter how hard they worked. Ashaninka hunters and fishermen could not bring in enough boar, ducks, turkeys and catfish to feed everyone, either. To do so would have soon depleted the wildlife in the jungles and rivers surrounding the town. At any length, service in the civilian militia occupied much of the farmers' time and the hunters had to save precious ammunition for the more urgent task of defending Poyeni against the Path. Everyone in the refugee towns downriver knew that, if Poyeni fell, Shining Path would have an open avenue on the Tambo. Those Ashaninka who knew how prayed that Poyeni would not fall.

Poyeni defenders organized a civilian militia under the guidance of the Peruvian military. The military did not supply the defenders with weapons, however. The Ashaninka used their own guns and bought their own bullets. That is, those who could afford to, bought bullets. Money was tight for many of the men defending Poyeni. The war had forced them to abandon their farms, leaving coffee and cacao crops unharvested. Many Ashaninka warriors used dart guns or bows and arrows, instead of rifles and shotguns, to defend Poyeni. From a military point of view, the odds were against an Ashaninka victory. The odds were four to one, in fact, taking into account the enemies they faced: poverty, hunger, over-population and the Path.

Some military factors did favour the Poyeni defenders, however. First, their position on the high bluff overlooking the Tambo gave them the ability to spot advancing enemy columns. Second, every time the *senderistas* attacked, they faced an exhausting climb up the steep cliffs. Third, a radio network established with Shevoja, Betania and a dozen other settlements downriver guaranteed that reinforcements would come to Poyeni's aid when necessary. Fourth, the Ashaninka were deft marksmen. From childhood they had used their rifles, shot-guns, darts, bows and arrows to hunt game in the hills of their homeland.

One more factor favoured the Ashaninka. Many of them knew how to pray. In fact, Alfonso Torribio led prayers every day in Poyeni. The 50-year-old Torribio had pastored the Ashaninka Evangelical Church in the village for nearly half his lifetime. Among the 2,000 refugees in Poyeni, some 800 were professing Christians. Torribio and his fellow pastors gathered the believers for daily fasting, prayer and Bible study. They knew as well as anybody that, given the odds against them, nothing short of a miracle would keep Poyeni from falling to the Path. 'Brothers came in from everywhere to help us,' Torribio later told a visiting journalist. 'But I knew that, without the help of God, we could not prevail.'

*   *   *

Alejandro Aurelio of Potsoteni, the clever man who made the Path drunk on *masato* so he could lead the midnight escape downriver on *balsas*, was the first Ashaninka defender to die in the Battle of Poyeni. One morning a few days after the first guerrilla attack, Aurelio and his wife Maria went hunting. Alejandro assumed, wrongly as it turned out, that the terrorists had abandoned the area following the unsuccessful assault. Aurelio shot a parrot that morning and the report of his gun evidently attracted a *senderista* patrol lurking in the hills. Maria managed to escape the ambush the terrorists laid for the couple and ran back to Poyeni to tell the civilian militia. They followed her back to the site of the ambush and found Alejandro's body. The militia searched for his killers, but to no avail. They returned sadly to Poyeni to caution the rest of the Ashaninka hunters to remain in the village and save their ammunition for a more urgent task.

On 2 October, once again at 6.00 a.m., the Path launched a second attack on Poyeni. This time, the defenders were better prepared. In the two weeks since the initial assault, the civilian militia had finished digging trenches around the perimeter of the town. Ashaninka marksmen could stand in the chest-high ditches and fire on attacking guerrillas through rocks piled along the outer rims of the holes. Defenders dug similar trenches under houses inside the village to hide the women and children. If the Path broke through the perimeter, the marksmen could fall back to these interior trenches and continue the fight.

Shining Path was better prepared this time, as well. In addition to machine guns, automatic weapons and dynamite, they brought fire bombs to hurl at the village. Several fires started among the cane and palm thatch homes of the Ashaninka, causing panic among the women and children hiding underneath. Two youngsters who bolted from the trenches were gunned down by the *senderistas*.

As the fighting wore on, casualties mounted, mostly on the side of the Path. Despite superior firepower, the guerrillas failed to subdue the village. Around 10 o'clock, just before reinforcements arrived from Shevoja, Betania and other Ashaninka settlements downriver, the terrorists withdrew. The retreat cost them yet more casualities. Their route back up the Tambo lay across the smaller Poyeni River. Since dawn, when they had first crossed the stream, a pouring rainstorm had turned the normally manageable Poyeni into a swollen torrent. When the *senderistas* plunged into it, the stream swept some of them away. Unable to swim and encumbered with weapons, the terrorists drowned.

By the time Ashaninka reinforcements arrived, there was little left for them to do except help the Poyeni defenders collect the corpses of the fallen *senderistas* and throw them into the river. The militiamen counted the casualties: 60 dead terrorists, an estimated 150 wounded. Among the Ashaninka themselves, four had died: the two children who tried to run from under the burning house and two civilian militia, José Vásquez and Elías Chiricente. The town held funeral services for the deceased at the Ashaninka Evangelical Church before burying them.

The Ashaninka had inflicted major damage on the Path, despite their use of ancient rifles, shotguns, darts, bows and arrows. What accounted for the tribes' lopsided success? Alfonso Torribio cited a number of reasons.

We had better aim. That's because, from childhood on, we learn how to hunt. Many of the *senderistas* did not shoot well because they got nervous. That didn't happen with us.

Also, my uncle and my brother killed some of them with arrows. We used dart guns, too. Usually when we hunt, we don't use poison. But we put poison on the tips so the *senderistas* would die faster.

Sometimes we ran out of ammunition. We had to count every shot. Some men had 20 shells, others only ten. So they had to be sure of every shot.

Food was nearly as scarce as bullets in Poyeni. The Catholic chaplaincy of San Ramón sent several shipments of emergency rations to the village, but supply could not keep up with demand. 'Many times, we had only manioc to eat,' Torribio said. 'The children nearly died of hunger.'

The Path waited three weeks before attacking Poyeni the third time. Again, they failed to defeat the defenders. But in this assault, the *senderistas* lost only three dead in the fighting. That was because the battle lasted only a brief time before the guerrillas found themselves obliged to retreat. The Path had run out of bullets.

*   *   *

Although Poyeni suffered the brunt of guerrilla attacks, the Ashaninka defending the village had one advantage: they could identify the enemy. That was not so easy to do in the areas the Path occupied on the Ene and upper Tambo Rivers. There, the revolutionaries mingled freely with other outsiders. One never knew, in fact, whether the stranger one was dealing with was a *senderista* or simply an outsider. The terrorists sometimes posed as civilians, or even civilian militia, to spy on the tribe. The Ashaninka, ever mistrustful of outsiders, now learned to trust them even less.

In time, Shining Path learned to mistrust everyone in the liberated zone, Ashaninka as well as outsiders. They learned that evangelical pastors in particular were no friends of the revolution. The pastors not only refused to join the struggle themselves, but the Ashaninka to whom they taught Bible lessons and led in prayer meetings also refused to join the revolution. Augosto Diaz, Pedro Aurelio and other pastors of the Ashaninka Evangelical Church became marked men. Some of them became martyrs.

When Maurine Friesen recalls the martyrs, her blue eyes fairly blaze. 'We heard about one or two churches that were crucified. One young man named Cisco was supposed to come out to enrol in the university. He had his papers, everything all ready. He went back to get his wife and they caught him. They took him to the river and tortured him with near drowning, wanting him to give up his faith. I think it was about three days. He wouldn't do it, so they drowned him.'

Initially, Shining Path believed the school teachers living in Tsiriari were sincere followers of the revolution. After the attack on the village that drove the Diaz family into the jungle, the guerrillas allowed four of the local teachers – outsiders who were working there on government contracts – to stay on and continue giving classes. In return, the teachers pledged to support the revolution. For the next two and half years, the educators lived in Tsiriari, teaching students from the village and some who came there for classes from surrounding communities. Sometimes the teachers held classes in outlying villages, many of which, like Tsiriari, were but gutted hamlets with a handful of inhabitants. It was on one of these visits that the Path discovered the teachers were not, after all, sincere followers of the revolution.

A group of Shining Path spies, living in the charred remains of a village and posing as civilian militia, made the discovery. One day, the Tsiriari teachers passed by and, believing the spies to be who they claimed, revealed to them their true opinions of Shining Path. The spies reported the comments to their commander, who decided the teachers were guilty of treason and deserved the full weight of revolutionary justice. At 6.00 p.m. on 9 August 1992, 30 armed terrorists moved into Tsiriari and gathered the community together. The teachers had no idea of the danger. They knew some of the *senderistas* personally, some were even relatives of their students. They expected to endure nothing worse than another long people's meeting. They were mistaken.

Next morning, Augosto Diaz's 15-year-old nephew Dino walked to the village for another day of classes. But the school in Tsiriari did not hold classes that day, nor for many days afterwards. Dino found his teacher lying dead in the road. The Path had cut the man's throat from ear to ear and split his torso from thorax to navel. Seventeen other persons lay dead in Tsiriari that morning, their bodies similarly mutilated. The *senderistas* had murdered four teachers, their families and some of the students from the secondary school. One 15-year-old girl reportedly died at the hands of her own cousin, who was ordered by the Path to administer the full weight of revolutionary justice.

*   *   *

Poyeni never succumbed to revolutionary justice. On the morning of 23 November 1992, 400 Shining Path guerrillas threw themselves against the entrenched Ashaninka defending the high bluff overlooking the Tambo. It would be the Path's last assault on the village. Civilian militia used their ancient rifles, shotguns, bows and arrows to deadly effect. Despite superior firepower, the *senderistas* were no match for the Ashaninka marksmen. By midmorning, scores of terrorists lay dead on the 500-foot cliff surrounding the village. Some made it to the summit, but turned and fled again in the face of a lethal barrage of bullets, arrows and poison darts. Some who fled too hastily fell down the steep cliff and perished.

By the time reinforcements arrived from the Ashaninka settlements downriver, there was little left for them to do but help the Poyeni defenders collect the corpses of *senderistas* and throw them into the river. There were so many this time, however, that the Ashaninka elected to leave many of the fallen terrorists lying where they died. In time, the jungle would consume the bodies. The Poyeni defenders tallied another lopsided casualty count: 150 Shining Path killed, four Ashaninka wounded. The battle for Poyeni had ended.

Shining Path could not afford to mount another assault on

the town. Following the fourth attack, the Peruvian Navy decided it would be prudent to establish a base on the strategic bend of the Tambo. The military presence freed Poyeni from the *senderista* threat. In fact, the feared guerrilla movement was rapidly imploding all over the country. At the same time at the end of 1992 that the Ashaninka were defeating the Path at Poyeni, army troops and civil defence forces were crushing *senderista* units in the Ayacucho highlands. After Presidente Gonzalo's capture in Lima that September, precise orders from the Path's high command had stopped coming down to local commanders, throwing field battalions into confusion. Squeezed between the angry Ashaninka and the advancing army, Shining Path forces began to withdraw from the central jungle, releasing their grip on the natives they held hostage.

The Troubles did not stop immediately, however, especially for the Ashaninka who lived along the Ene and upper Tambo Rivers where scattered bands of *senderistas* still roamed. The Ernesto family of Puerto Ashaninka, for instance, suffered Shining Path captivity for two years more, wandering from one guerrilla camp to another, forced to work for the revolution. They gained their freedom only when an argument arose between their *senderista* overlords. The squabble ended in a gunfight in which several terrorists killed each other. The Ernesto family and their neighbours slipped away and returned home.

For nearly a year following the decisive Ashaninka victory at Poyeni, the village of Otica, far up the Tambo, continued to live under the spell of Shining Path. A handful of *senderistas* controlled the town through tyranny and lies about a pending Shining Path victory. Otica endured isolation, hunger and disease. Then one day, half the *senderistas* left the town to spy on Ashaninka communities downriver and the other half headed upriver to seek supplies. The terrorists left three Ashaninka men whom they assumed to be sincere followers of the revolution in charge of the village. As soon as the terrorists were gone, two of the leaders proposed an escape. When the third protested, they cut his throat. Paul Friesen later learned of the incident from one of the Ashaninka himself. 'That was my own brother we had to kill, because he wouldn't let us go,' the man said sadly. 'When he was out of the way, we went by boat to Poyeni, 128 people in all. When the *senderistas* came back, they had no more people, so they just left.'

By early 1994, the Path had completely abandoned the territory around Otica and the refugees could safely return home to rebuild their farms and homes. That September, Ashaninka militia used Otica as a base to explore territory further up the Ene River. They found the hills virtually free of guerrillas. A contingent of men resettled in the village of Centro Caperocía to rebuild their homes, clear land and sow manioc, yams and bananas. By December, the men had put things in order so that their families could join them. At the behest of Torribio Alfonso, military helicopters flew their wives and children from Poyeni to Centro Caperocía to complete the resettlement.

However, the families had little time to relish reunion. Two weeks after the arrival of the women and children, 150 emaciated Ashaninka emerged from the jungle where they had been hiding from the Path and asked for asylum in Centro Caperocía. The village was ill-prepared for the newcomers. The manioc and yams the men had planted would not be ready for weeks. The food they had brought with them was just enough to get them through to harvest. Nevertheless, they shared what they had with the refugees. Mostly they shared hunger. But they were Ashaninka, after all, and Ashaninka know how to share. Otherwise, they would not have survived the Troubles.

To a greater or lesser degree, the Troubles left an indelible mark on Ashaninka communities. After Shining Path withdrew, Tsiriari managed to rebuild itself quickly, thanks to its favourable location on the main road between Mazamari and Puerto Ocopa. Augosto Diaz moved his family back home to Tsiriari from Betania and resumed his ministry as pastor of the Ashaninka Evangelical Church there. On the other hand, Pablo Cecilio and his wife Natividad will likely never return to Alto Gloriabamba to pastor the church there. In fact, the Ashaninka Evangelical Church has not reopened in Alto Gloriabamba, nor in dozens of other Ashaninka settlements. Alto Gloriabamba itself has not yet rebuilt, nor have dozens of other Ashaninka settlements.

At her new home in Puerto Ocopa, Natividad explained to a visiting journalist what happened after her husband surrendered to the army, following his daring escape from the Path.

'He was confined for two weeks here in the stockade. My children came every day to visit their father until his release. Since that time, we have lived in Puerto Ocopa, next door to my uncle. We gave up our 20 acres of coffee in Alto Gloriabamba. Now we cultivate five acres on community land here. The coffee will soon start producing. Meanwhile, the kids are studying. One is already in secondary school and the rest are about to finish primary.'

Those who know their story believe there are several reasons why the Ashaninka survived the Troubles and triumphed over the Path. One, they were fighting on their own land, against outsiders unfamiliar with life in the jungle. Two, their tribal school system and the Ashaninka Evangelical Church provided a strong social network that bound them together in the midst of the crisis. Three, the Ashaninka are adept warriors. The battle for Poyeni proved, in extraordinary fashion, that their reputation as such is well deserved.

But should you ask Paul and Maurine Friesen, or Mrs Natividad Cecilio, or Torribio Alfonso about why the tribe prevailed over the Path and the Troubles, they will tell you it was because those Ashaninka who knew how to prayed.

11

Lawyer of lawyers

The night the security police took their parents away to DINCOTE headquarters in Lima, 14-year-old Rodolfo Jaimes, his sister Kelly, 11, their brother Lorenzo, nine, and sister Carlita, aged two and a half, remained home alone, frightened and confused.

'We thought that they were taking them for interrogation and that they would come right home again,' Rodolfo said. 'Mama and Papa even took money for bus fares with them. We stayed in the house by ourselves all the next day, sad, but expecting our parents to return in the evening. That did not happen. We were still waiting for them when some Christians came and explained to us that their case was serious.'

'It was terrible, terrible,' Kelly said. 'We did not understand what was happening. The neighbours asked me if it were true that a car bomb had left our house. I said, of course not, never. We cried and cried. We wanted only to see Papa and Mama again. They should not have taken them from us like that in the middle of the night.'

Benito and Antonia Jaimes did not return home that evening, nor the next. In fact, had any of the Jaimes family known how long it would be before parents and children would see each other again, the fear and confusion would have been unbearable.

Antonia folds her worn hands on the table at the Peace and Hope office and continues the story.

We were kept at DINCOTE for one month and a fortnight. All the people who came to see me said I need only make a statement and they would let me go. When I asked the officers about this, they said, 'We know nothing about your case. The public prosecutor is going to try you before a civil court.' What we did not know was that, before our arrest, the police had captured a terrorist with a car bomb in our neighbourhood. They forced him to name his accomplices, so he took them to our street, pointed to our house and said it was the place he built the car bomb. The police never told us about this, nor did they reveal the identity of the terrorist. Only later did we learn his name: Guillermo Flores Rivera.

One day they took us to a room and had my husband sign a paper. They took me to another table and had me put my fingerprint on two different papers. Since I did not know how to read and write, I didn't know what I was doing. Later, an officer told me that signing these papers sent our case before a military tribunal.

There the judge said to me, 'Why have you signed a statement admitting that your are a terrorist?'

'On the contrary,' I said, 'I signed a statement so that I could be released. I've had nothing to do with terrorists.'

'It says here that you signed a confession in the DINCOTE office.'

'That is a lie.'

They sentenced us to life imprisonment. The only thing I could say was, 'Your honour, I have four young children. Please, do not do this. If not for my sake, at least for theirs. I am innocent.'

A lawyer was there and said that I should appeal. I didn't know what an appeal was. They took me to Chorrillos prison and my husband to Castro Castro. My children were split up. Rodolfo went to live with a brother-in-law, Lorenzo with another brother-in-law, Kelly and Carlita with my sister-in-law. The stress and anxiety hurt them. Rodolfo dropped out of school and went to work in construction with his uncle. Kelly took a job as a maid. We would be gone nearly four years.

*   *   *

There in the prison, they told me, 'You are never going to leave. You will die here. I said, 'I am not going to die. I have a lawyer of lawyers. He is going to get me out of here. It won't be tomorrow, nor the next day, but my freedom is coming. I have confidence in him.'

I pleaded with God, 'Lord, send me a sister who can help me understand your Word.' Shortly afterward, a woman named Teófila Curi was imprisoned. At 5.00 in the morning she was singing praises. I got up and listened closely to songs that by now I had forgotten. When they let us out into the patio, I said, 'Señora, are you an evangelical?'

'Yes, I am.' She showed me her Bible. The words of the choruses were written inside the back cover.

'I don't know how to read or write,' I said. 'I would like for you to teach me.'

'That would be fine.'

Sometime later, Colonel Cornejo Coveña came through the cell block. I had never spoken to the Colonel because I was afraid. The rules were quite strict. I asked the Lord to give me words in that instant.

'Colonel, one moment please. I would like to speak with you.'

'You have a problem?'

'No, sir. I just would like to ask if Teófila Curi from cell three could move to our cell. I don't know how to read and I would like for her to read the Bible to me.'

'Who here is Teófila Curi?' the Colonel asked.

'I am.'

'What do you say? Will you move to Antonia's cell?'

'If you say so, Colonel. The Bible says that we ought to respect those in authority over us.'

From then on, we would rise in the early hours of the morning to sing hymns and pray. 'Today, Lord, take the blinds from my eyes so that I can read,' I would ask, clinging to the cell bars. 'I want to know about you, Lord. Teach me. Your Word says: "Call to me and I will answer you, and will tell you great and hidden things which you have not known."' That is how I learned to read. My family is my witness.

My sister-in-law did not allow the children to come to visit me because I had been sentenced to life imprisonment. They thought I would be there until I was an old woman. Thanks to Ms Gabriela Hope, a human rights counsellor, I was able to see my daughter, Kelly, two years following our arrest. She was 14 years old when she came to Chorrillos prison for the first visit.

'Are you Kelly?' I asked.

'I am,' she replied.

I did not recognize her. She had grown quite tall. I thought she was one of my sister-in-law's children.

'Mama, I'm working to put some money together and hire a lawyer to take your case,' she said. 'Then, when I grow up, I'm going to study law and become a lawyer myself. I'm going to get both you and Papa out of here.'

*   *   *

On a day in April 1994, Peace and Hope attorney José Regalado stood in the thin air, staring in exasperation at the dull walls of Yanomayo Maximum Security Prison. Regalado had travelled 750 miles from his home in Lima and ascended 12,600 feet to Peru's cold, wind-swept *altiplano* with the sole intention of getting inside those walls. Now it appeared his trip would end in vain. The commanding officer of Yanomayo had refused Regalado admittance, citing security regulations. 'We have the most dangerous terrorists in Peru incarcerated here,' the major said. 'It is impossible for you to have contact with them.'

The only Yanomayo prisoner José sought to contact was Juan Carlos Chuchón. A native of San Francisco de Pujas, near Ayacucho, Juan Carlos had worked as a bricklayer in Lima for nearly ten years before beginning a 30-year sentence in Yanomayo for treason against the state. His wife, Pelagia Salcedo Chuchón, was also imprisoned, in Chorrillos, serving 30 years for the same crime. Both were arrested the same night in December 1992 in a police raid on their modest home in the Lima suburb of Canto Grande. Both were tried and convicted by a military tribunal within one month of their arrest. Both, José Regalado believed, were innocent.

Regalado had been trying to make contact with Juan Carlos Chuchón for weeks, ever since Peace and Hope had received a letter from leaders of the Assemblies of God of Peru affirming that the couple were long-standing members of their church, had no dealings whatsoever with Shining Path and had suffered grave injustice at the hands of the authorities. The letter had confirmed the statement of a fellow inmate, Miguel Cornejo. In a televized press conference, Cornejo declared that an innocent man named Chuchón had been unjustly imprisoned in Yanomayo, where he spent his time organizing Bible groups and prayer meetings. The evidence persuaded the staff of Peace and Hope to help the Chuchón family, pending, as was policy, a personal interview with the accused. That was why José Regalado stood today outside the dull walls of the prison high on the windswept *altiplano*.

While he stood there, José prayed. He told God that, frankly, he was irritated. 'Why did you have me come all this way, only to return home empty-handed?' Just then, the police radio crackled with a message for the commanding officer. He hurried away towards nearby Lake Titicaca in his official car, leaving his second-in-command, a captain, in charge. After a few minutes the captain struck up a conversation.

'You are an evangelical Christian, aren't you?'

'Yes, I am,' José replied.

'Would you mind answering some questions about the Bible for me?'

José said he would be delighted to talk about whatever the captain had on his mind. The captain's questions seemed to involve a marital problem, so José showed the officer some texts of scripture dealing with relationships between husband and wife. The man listened intently. When José had finished, he said, 'Say, Dr Regalado, would you like to enter the prison to visit some of your Christian brothers?'

'I would like that very much. In particular, I want to see Juan Carlos Chuchón.'

Within moments, prison guards were ushering José through a series of iron doors, each one locked and guarded. At length he found himself standing in a narrow passage, facing a wall of thick steel grating. A moment later, he realized that Juan Carlos Chuchón stood on the other side of the wall, peering at him through the mesh of heavy wire. José introduced himself and Chuchón burst into tears.

'Thank you, Lord, thank you!' he cried.'You sent one of your children.'

José Regalado stood stock still, unable to speak.'When I saw Juan Carlos Chuchón for the first time, I was struck dumb,' he later told a journalist. 'I am no Pentecostal. I'm a member of the Alliance Church, which has quite formal beliefs. Yet in that moment, I felt the touch of the Spirit of God. I started to weep, I was trembling. For ten minutes I could not articulate one word. I just stood there with Juan Carlos and we cried together. It was the first time he had had a visitor.'

When Juan Carlos was able to talk, the first thing he wanted to discuss was what God was doing inside the Yanomayo Maximum Security Prison. He told José that ten men on his cell block had accepted Christ since he began daily Bible groups. 'My brother, their only hope, their only consolation in here is the Word of God. I've asked the Lord to help me preach the gospel to these people. I want to be an instrument of God in this prison.'

José and Juan then discussed the harsh conditions in which prisoners in Yanomayo lived. Due to the extreme altitude, the inmates endured constant cold in their unheated cells. Strict security regulations and the huge distance from home limited family visits. Censors read all correspondence and confiscated letters deemed suspicious. José noted the needs. His wife Ruth and the rest of the Peace and Hope staff would collect sweaters and other warm clothing for the Yanomayo inmates, he promised, as well as Bibles. Peace and Hope would also contact the international network of Christians who were concerned about the plight of the prisoners and ask them to write letters to Juan Carlos Chuchón and other Yanomayo inmates. Prison censors would soon have lots more correspondence to read.

'What left the greatest impression on me,' José said later, 'was that this brother did not say, "You must do something for me, resolve my case." Nothing of the sort. He did mention that other Christian brothers were in jail there and, please, would I keep asking people to pray for the innocent, that prayer was of great value. From that moment on, this case absorbed my attention. I could not stop thinking about it.

'I returned to Lima and shared my findings with the Peace and Hope Commission. Our office contacted Mrs Pelagia Chuchón in Chorrillos prison and found she had helped organize a church behind bars. We began legal investigations and, truly, this was a case of gross miscarriage of justice.'

*   *   *

3.00 a.m., Friday, 11 December 1992

Pelagia was the first one awakened by the barking dogs and the footsteps on the roof. 'Juan, listen!' she said to her husband sleeping beside her. 'Someone is trying to get in.'

Juan mumbled something incoherent. Exhausted from a day of bricklaying, he did not rouse easily at this time of night. Pelagia threw off the bed covers, ran to the sitting room and flipped the light switch. Nothing happened. The intruders had cut the electricity. A shadow lurking under the stairs to the roof startled Pelagia.

'Thief! Thief!' she screamed.

The shadow swore at her. 'Shut up! I'm a police officer.' He pointed his gun at Pelagia. 'Shut up and don't move!'

At that instant, Juan burst through the door with a chair in his hands, ready to strike the intruder. A second shadow pointed a gun at him and growled, 'Drop it or I'll kill you.'

The policemen slipped a hood over Juan's head, pushed him down into the chair, tied him to it and kicked it over. 'Stand there facing the wall,' they ordered Pelagia. 'Don't take your eyes off it.'

By then, the two Chuchón children, eight-year-old Marlene and Avilio, 13, were awake. When they entered the room, the intruders grabbed Avilio, threw a hood over his head and forced him to the floor beside his father.

'Go stand by your mother,' they told Marlene. 'Don't look at her, keep your eyes on the wall.'

'But, what is happening?' Pelagia asked, and started to cry. Without answering, the intruders started ransacking the Chuchón house. It went on for hours. At one point, Pelagia realized, they found the family's identification papers. She heard them whispering among themselves. 'Look, it says here they originally came from Ayacucho. These people must be terrorists.' Later, she discerned sounds of digging in the back yard, where Juan had dumped a pile of sand left over from a construction job. She could not see what they were doing, of course, because a man held a gun at her back to ensure that she did not take her eyes off the wall. Finally, they told her to turn around. In the grey light of dawn she saw heavily armed and masked men in police uniforms holding an odd yellow bag in their hands.

'We found this bag buried in the sand pile out back,' they said. Pelagia knew they meant to do her family more harm than any thief.

'Why are you doing this to us?' she pleaded. 'Have we offended you somehow? We have never had anything to do with terrorism, ever. Our whole life is working, raising our children. We have never supported the terrorists. In fact, they tried to kill us once.'

'Can you identify this bag?' they asked her.

'Look at this bag, it's clean and dry,' Pelagia pleaded. 'If you had taken it out of that sand pile, it would be full of mud because that's where I empty my cleaning water every day.'

The masked men cursed and struck her across the face. 'You're a terrorist!' they shouted. They dumped the contents of the yellow bag on the table: a few sticks of dynamite, guns and hand grenades, old and rusted. Even Pelagia could see that these weapons did not belong to any serious terrorist. The police thrust a paper before her.

'You will sign here, stating that we found these items on these premises,' they told Pelagia.

'I will do no such thing,' she protested. 'I have never seen those things in my life.'

'Honey, don't sign any papers!' Juan blurted from under the hood. The policemen kicked him and beat him with gun butts, shouting, 'Shut up, you terrorist!' When they finished, they pointed the guns at Pelagia. One man shoved a ballpoint pen into her hand, another grabbed a fistful of her hair and snapped her head back.

'Sign this paper,' he growled. 'If not, we will kill your kids.'

Pelagia could hear Marlene sobbing, still standing by the wall. 'Mama, sign the paper! They're going to kill us!'

Pelagia clenched her teeth and closed her eyes. The hand of a policeman clamped over hers and guided the ballpoint pen across the page.

*   *   *

During their investigation of the Chuchón case, the Peace and Hope defence team developed a compelling theory as to why Juan Carlos and Pelagia, two respectable, hard-working people, should suddenly find themselves imprisoned for 30 years. The theory turned upon an age-old human vice – revenge.

The events leading up to the Chuchóns' arrest were set in motion more than ten years earlier, when the Path first invaded the couple's hometown of San Francisco de Pujas and murdered a wealthy landowner named Medina at his *hacienda* outside town. Villagers learned of the atrocity when a police squadron arrived in San Francisco de Pujas and requested their help in apprehending the murderers. Juan Carlos, who was a town councillor at the time, joined the posse. They succeeded in tracking the *senderistas* to their hideout, but arrested only two suspects. The main fighting force was absent from camp at the time. Three months later, the guerrillas returned to San Francisco de Pujas to punish the town for cooperating with the authorities. They killed the late Mr Medina's son-in-law, who had moved into the large *hacienda* outside town, along with the police squadron guarding it, then rounded up what town councillors they could find and executed them in the main plaza. Juan Carlos got wind of the terrorist attack in time to escape into the surrounding mountains. From there, he travelled on to Lima. As soon as he found lodgings and work, Pelagia and little Avilio joined him.

The young family lived quietly among hundreds of thousands of other war refugees until 1992, the year Alberto Fujimori dictated strict anti-terrorist laws. According to Peace and Hope's theory, one of the *senderistas* from San Francisco de Pujas who was behind bars and, therefore, unable to settle scores with Juan Carlos personally, used the new anti-terrorist laws to effect revenge. Thus, Juan Carlos, who once had risked his life to fight terrorism, was now in prison as a convicted terrorist. This was but part of the obscene irony. By accusing Juan Carlos and Pelagia of membership of Shining Path, their old enemy also succeeded in reducing his own prison sentence. The 'repented terrorist' clause allowed *senderistas* to do this at no risk to themselves, since it forbade police from divulging the name of the accuser to the accused. The Chuchóns would never know who was responsible for sending them to jail. In the end it did not matter anyway.

It did matter that the staff of Peace and Hope believed in the Chuchóns' innocence and came to their aid. The first step in the legal battle involved appealing against their conviction. A non-governmental organization known as the Institute of Legal Defence undertook the appeal, with support from Peace and Hope. The defence team asked the court to overturn the verdict of the military tribunal, citing gross errors in the police investigation. Officers had not secured a search warrant before raiding the Chuchón home, nor had a public prosecutor signed the arrest order until after the police had taken the couple into custody. Also, a medical examiner had discovered marks of a serious beating inflicted on both Juan Carlos and Pelagia, which indicated the police had obtained their confession by force. In normal cases, this evidence alone would have compelled the court to overturn the Chuchón conviction. But this was no normal case, rather, a trial before faceless judges conducted under anti-terrorist law. The appeal was denied.

The defence team had expected it to be denied, as were most appeals involving military trials before faceless judges. In the end, it did not matter anyway, because help for Juan Carlos and Pelagia Chuchón would come from another quarter.

*   *   *

Following her trial and imprisonment, Pelagia Chuchón scored a major victory against the system. She recovered her Bible. Upon arrival at the Chorrillos women's prison, the authorities had taken it away from her, along with everything else she owned.

'Security regulations,' they said. 'No books, pencils or paper allowed inside.'

'But I need my Bible in order to converse with God,' Pelagia pleaded through tears.

'Impossible,' they said. 'Nobody here has a Bible. They're all *senderistas*.'

'Please, God, touch the heart of the person in charge here,' Pelagia prayed after they had put her in the cell. 'Make them give me back my Bible.'

Next day the colonel passed through the corridor on inspection. When he reached her cell, Pelagia said, 'Please, sir, my Bible is at the door outside. Could you see that I get it?'

The colonel looked at Pelagia, but said nothing. He continued his inspection. Pelagia continued her prayers. The officer reached the cell block door, hesitated, then turned and came back to Pelagia's cell.

'What were you saying to me?' he said.

'My Bible, it was taken from me at the door yesterday. It has my name in it: Mrs Pelagia Salcedo Chuchón. Please, sir, may I have it?'

The colonel sighed. 'Lady, since you insist, I'll see to it.' He turned and left. A few minutes later he returned with the Bible.

The rest of the inmates took notice of the incident. 'Who are you, some queen?' they said to Pelagia. 'You surely have some kind of pull. Let's see your crown.'

'It's not me,' Pelagia told them, 'it's the power of God.'

Many of the Chorrillos inmates, committed *senderistas* that they were, did not believe in God. But when Pelagia Chuchón, Teófila Curi, Antonia Jaimes and other Christians imprisoned in Chorrillos began to share the gospel with them, they showed interest. In fact, Pelagia was soon reading her Bible daily to the inmates in Chorrillos, just as her husband Juan Carlos was reading the Bible daily to inmates in Yanomayo.

After a time, Chorrillos inmates showed such interest in the gospel that authorities allowed three Christian workers, Norma Hinojosa, Angélica Flores and Maureen Galloway to conduct weekly worship services in the prison.

This came about after Pelagia received a visit from Peace and Hope attorney José Regalado. José told her that he had been to Yanomayo to see her husband and that Peace and Hope was helping defend the two of them against the terrorism charges.

'This is going to be difficult,' he said. 'The military has placed your case file in its legal archives, which means it is officially closed and cannot be reopened. But don't lose hope. The Lord God is our hope. He is helping us.'

An important part of the help the Lord sent Pelagia and Juan Carlos came through their own daughter. The police raid on their modest home that December night had traumatized Marlene Chuchón, as it would have traumatized any eight-year-old. Marlene endured further trauma seeing her mother behind bars when her Aunt Benedicta, with whom she and her brother now lived, took her and Avilio to Chorrillos for their first visit. Security regulations restricted visits to one day every three months, which further heightened the trauma for the Chuchón children. Avilio, in fact, stopped visiting his mother after the second trip because someone told the boy that he would be jailed as a terrorist himself if he went there again. Neither child ever had an opportunity to visit their father in far-off Yanomayo.

Despite the trauma, Marlene earnestly declared her parents' innocence to anyone willing to listen: neighbours, school mates, even the policemen who arrested them and the judges who convicted them. The judges did not accept Marlene's testimony, however, because she was under-age and a relative and therefore, according to anti-terrorist law, an unfit witness. But when Peace and Hope assumed her parents' defence, Marlene got the opportunity to declare her parents' innocence on television. The team arranged for the girl, who had turned 11 by then, to appear on a news programme with her Aunt Benedicta. She told of the night strangers broke into their home, bound and beat her parents, spilled a bag of old guns and dynamite on the family table and forced her mother to sign a paper saying she was a Shining Path terrorist. It was not the first time Marlene had told the story, but it was the first time that adults took her seriously. The experience so impressed the little girl she decided that, when she grew up, she would become a journalist.

'But I'm going to be a good journalist,' she told her mother on a visit to the Chorrillos prison. 'I want to help the people in jail who are innocent and who've left children behind who need them. I want to see justice done.'

The TV testimonies of Marlene and her Aunt Benedicta were not, in themselves, sufficient to acquit her parents of terrorist charges. Yet, the media exposure played an important role in Peace and Hope's strategy for freeing the Chuchóns, along with other innocent Peruvians likewise imprisoned. Alfonso Wieland and his team knew that public opinion, if forceful enough, was the one thing that could convince Peruvian politicians to redress the tragic injustices brought on by the anti-terrorist laws decreed in 1992. Peace and Hope marshalled substantial public opinion through the worldwide network of concerned Christian organizations. Peruvian politicians could not ignore the thousands of letters from Switzerland, Holland, the United Kingdom, Canada, the USA and elsewhere urging them to resolve the cases of innocent persons in prison.

What finally freed Juan Carlos and Pelagia Chuchón from prison, along with scores of other innocent Peruvians, was the Law of Pardon 26655. Approved by the National Congress on 15 August 1996, the law created an independent commission to review the cases of persons accused of treason against the state and recommend full pardon for those wrongfully convicted. The Law of Pardon marked a major victory for the Christians who had laboured so hard on behalf of the innocent. The text of the new legislation even acknowledged those labours, citing the 'valiant efforts' of the National Council of Evangelicals of Peru and the Catholic Episcopal Commission on Social Action as a 'decisive factor' leading to the passage of the Law of Pardon 26655.

Despite the accolades, Alfonso Wieland and the rest of the

Peace and Hope team knew that the decisive factor in this victory was not of their doing.

'This law,' Alfonso told a journalist the day the law passed, 'is an answer to the prayers of thousands of Christians, within Peru as well as around the world.'

*   *   *

Friday, 4 October 1996

Though she did not know it, today would be the last day Mrs Antonia Jaimes spent in Chorrillos prison.

One fine morning – I will never forget it – very early I was lying face down on my bunk reading my Bible. Just then the Colonel came and stood at the cell door. 'Good morning, Antonia.'

'Good morning, Colonel.'

'How are you?'

'I'm content, happy, thanks to our Lord Jesus Christ.'

'If you're so happy, then collect your things. You're leaving.'

'I'm leaving, Colonel?'

'The order for your release just arrived. Do you want to go or not? If you don't want to, no problem.'

'Is this for real, Colonel?'

'Yes, it's for real.'

I didn't know whether to shout or get down on my knees. 'Lord, you are no statue, you are Spirit,' I said. 'You have given me my freedom, Lord.' I cried and then I collected my things. They led me out to the front gate and there stood my lawyer, Dr Pilar Aguilar of the Catholic Episcopal Commission on Social Action.

'Antonia,' she said, 'tell the kids not to worry, their papa is going to get out soon, as well. He will have to wait a couple of weeks, maybe a month, but he will be freed. Now that you are acquitted, it will be easier for him.'

The reporters had arrived, a whole crowd of them. The guards and the young women there in the office said to me:

'It's true, Antonia, that you have called upon a living God. He has given you everything you asked.'

That same October morning, Mrs Pelagia Chuchón left Chorrillos prison along with Antonia Jaimes. Both were freed by the Law of Pardon 26655. In far-off Puno, Juan Carlos Chuchón emerged from the dull walls of Yanomayo Maximum Security Prison and left the windswept *altiplano* for a family reunion in Lima. It would be a fine reunion, the first for the Chuchón family in four long years.

While they stood at the gate of Chorrillos prison, Antonia, Pelagia and two other pardoned inmates, Santa Flores and Emeteria Quispe, answered reporters' questions and posed for photographs. These would be the first pictures published of innocent prisoners freed under the Law of Pardon.

'What's that you have in your hands?' a photographer asked the women.

'This is what gave us back our freedom,' they said.

'Hold it up so we can see it,' he said.

The picture he took later appeared in newspapers and on magazine covers across Peru. It was a fine photograph, too. It showed four worn but happy women, grinning from ear to ear and holding high their Bibles.

12

Forgiven

That day over lunch at the Christian and Missionary Alliance Church in Chorrillos when Jorge Rios asked Bruce and Jan Benson for forgiveness, what the ex-*senderista* got was a hearty bear hug from both missionaries and a tearful 'Of course!' 'We are your brother and sister in Christ now,' Bruce told the young man. Jorge did not fully comprehend what Bruce meant by that, nor did he understand why the Bensons were willing to help him get his life started again. But they did.

'As a guerrilla, I trusted nobody,' he later said. 'Comparing myself to other Christians in Lima, I would have ranked as the absolute least trustworthy of them all. But despite my never having done anything good, these people took great interest in helping me, with money, with advice about the basics of living. The Benson family was key to my Christian growth.'

Over the next few months, Jorge paid many visits to the Benson home for long talks and Bible study sessions. Bruce and Jan seemed to know exactly what Jorge needed to get his life started again. 'He couldn't hold a job because he didn't have any documents,' Bruce explained. 'He worked for churches in return for a room to stay in, but people were really kind of afraid of him. They didn't want to get too close, for fear of what might happen, either to him or to them.'

It bothered Jorge that Christians he met in Lima distrusted him, but they had their reasons. More than one evangelical pastor had discovered a Shining Path spy posing as a member of the church in order to gather intelligence for the terrorist movement. In other cases, 'repented' terrorists claimed conversion to Christ and joined themselves to local congregations. However, their behaviour revealed that their desire to serve the Lord was not nearly as genuine as their desire to avoid jail.

Jorge agonized over the fact that many of his new friends suspected him of being a hypocrite, or worse.

The Bensons agonized with Jorge. 'He'd call us frequently, really discouraged,' Jan said. 'He would say, "I'm going to go back to Tingo María, back to the jungle. At least I can work on a farm somewhere out there and they will give me something to eat." He hated being dependent on people. Then, all these things he had done would come back to haunt him and he would wonder if God could really forgive him.'

Thanks to the Bensons' friendship and counsel, Jorge eventually overcame his bouts of depression. And thanks to a part-time job the Christian and Missionary Alliance Church in San Agustín gave him, he eventually recovered his dignity. The congregation had opened a soup kitchen to help feed the thousands of immigrants who were flooding into the Lima area to escape the Path. The job represented a splendid irony. A former Shining Path revolutionary suddenly found himself cooking hot meals every morning for refugees of the revolution.

Jorge left work at 1 o'clock each day, but not to rest. He generally spent afternoons and evenings preaching, but not in churches. Street corners, plazas and city buses were his typical venues.

> A passion for people awoke within me. I could not be still, sitting around knowing that many of them did not know Christ. The assurance that Christ had forgiven me caused me such joy. To see people convert to Christ in the buses and in the plazas, that was my satisfaction.
>
> My convictions in Christ were growing deeper with every passing day. While still a young believer, I formed some perspective on the Christian life. I liked going to church. I faithfully attended every worship service. But I began to see that the church merely wanted to feel God's peace for itself. It showed little interest in people who did not know Christ.
>
> I proposed in my heart to be more than a good church member. To leave a revolution simply to sing choruses and listen to a sermon every Sunday made no sense to me. That

was only a drop in the bucket compared to what I could be doing.

I developed a particularly deep disquiet for Christian youth. At a time Peru was falling to pieces, killing itself in a revolution, young people who knew Christ, the only alternative for Peruvian society, were wasting their time on less important matters. This attitude of indifference repelled me. I began to talk with my pastor about my disenchantment.

Jorge also talked long hours with Bruce and Jan Benson about his disenchantment. 'Jorge, we feel strongly that you need a really good discipleship course,' they suggested. 'We know just the one.'

The Bensons told the young man about Youth With a Mission. YWAM, as the organization is commonly known, offered a six-month training course in discipleship and mission at YWAM bases around the world. Jan was herself an alumna of a discipleship school, completing the training in Hawaii before marrying Bruce. With Jorge's permission, she contacted YWAM bases in Argentina, Chile and Colombia to see if they had a place for him. Argentina was the first to respond, accepting Jorge for its next training session, which commenced six weeks hence.

In order to accept the YWAM invitation, Jorge needed two things: a passport and tuition money. The odds were long against his obtaining either in time to enrol in the school. 'One needs at least a year to acquire all the necessary travel documents,' he told the Bensons. 'The duplicate military discharge certificate takes three months. Then comes the voter registry, which takes another three months. You must have that in hand before applying for a passport, which takes six months to process. Why, it's impossible to obtain my papers in a month and a half.'

Bruce and Jan suggested Jorge try anyway. They even offered to buy him air passage to Iquitos, so that he could apply for the documents in his home town. 'We have a friend in Iquitos who works with the military, perhaps she can help,' they said. The friend did help, in fact, arranging for an army colonel to interview Jorge on the young man's first morning in town. After talking with Jorge, the officer processed his military discharge certificate by lunch time. That afternoon, Jorge obtained his voter registry with similar dispatch. By noon the second day, he had his passport in hand. The amazed young man stood gazing at the passport, tangible evidence of a bureaucratic miracle. He realized that God really did want him in Argentina.

The trip to Iquitos provided Jorge with another wondrous experience. He visited his parents, brothers and sisters for the first time since leaving home eight years before. His arrival created quite a stir, since the last news his family had of Jorge indicated that he died in Tingo María at the hands of the security forces. Jorge told the family of his conversion to Christ and the change that had come about in his life. They listened respectfully. Then he told them of his plans to travel to Argentina. 'No! you can't go,' they said. 'We don't even want you to return to Lima. It's too dangerous!' Jorge said that, danger or no, he must go. He had made a solemn promise to God. A week later and despite their pleas, Jorge bade his family an emotional goodbye.

Back in Lima, he stayed with the Bensons while making final preparations for Argentina. Between them, the three scraped together enough money to buy a bus ticket to Buenos Aires. However, when the day came for Jorge to leave on the three-day journey to the Argentine capital, none of them had the slightest idea how they would raise the money he needed to complete the six-month YWAM course. Jorge left anyway. While he was en route, the Bensons received a fax from missionary friends who had recently returned to Canada from Peru. During a brief visit on the eve of their friends' departure, Bruce and Jan had mentioned Jorge's plan and asked the couple to pray for his financial needs. They did. Their first week in Canada, the missionary couple spoke to a church in a town they had never before visited. They told of Jorge and his plans. Afterwards a woman they had never before met came up and handed them a cheque, explaining that God had told her it was for Jorge. The cheque was for 1,000 dollars, exactly enough to pay for the six-month YWAM course. The friends immediately faxed the news to the Bensons. Bruce and Jan stood gazing at the fax, tangible evidence of a financial miracle. They too realized that God really did want Jorge in Argentina.

*   *   *

When I was first converted, I began to grasp, in a very graphic sense, all the evil I had done. I wept constantly, asking God for forgiveness. In my mind, I continually saw men who had died. Friends in whose homes I spent the night and, just after I left in the early morning hours, the army arrived and killed them. A lot of children were left without parents because of me. When I arrived in Argentina, I asked God to give me just one chance in my life to preach Christ to those people.

In June of 1993, Pastor Ruben Matías moved to the city of Huánuco. I returned to Peru with the idea of asking forgiveness from the townspeople there. I planned to go only to Huánuco, but not to Tingo María. That would be much too dangerous. I reached Pastor Matías's home and we had a fine reunion. Afterward he started to tell me things.

'Everybody thinks you're dead. There has been a lot of talk, that they found you cut to pieces. Some say they saw your body dumped in the bush. A lot of people were happy when they heard the soldiers had killed you. I've only told a few trusted brothers that you are still alive.'

Then the pastor said to me, 'Say, why don't we bring the truth to light? Why don't we hold an evangelistic campaign in San Jorge?'

So I returned to the place where I was converted, to hold a three-day campaign. It was tremendous. The first night I was to preach, I went directly to speak with Efraín, my former bodyguard. At the time I was arrested and the soldiers supposedly killed me, this man turned himself in. The army gave him a *carte blanche*, which meant he could shoot anyone who he knew had participated, directly or indirectly, in Shining Path. He commanded the civilian militia in the village now.

I and another brother entered his house, but he could not

believe I was still alive. I said, 'Efraín, you know very well that I loved the revolution, that I had no fear of dying. I trained you to fight. I know that you are on the side of the army now and you have orders to shoot anyone who had contact with the Path. I am here, unarmed. If I had little reason to fear death before, I have even less now that I am a Christian. I did not betray anyone. I only joined another army, one that's worth fighting for.'

I talked to him about the love of God. This large, muscular man stood up and said, 'If your former life as a revolutionary had an impact on me, now it's even greater. I want you to pray for me.'

In that moment, Efraín gave his life to Jesus. The soldiers stood there and watched him cry. He said to me, 'Five miles from here, there is a battalion of guerrillas that is preparing to attack San Jorge. I will station all my sentries in the centre of town to guard your campaign. That way you can preach as many days as you like. There will be no problems.'

So I preached. First, I asked forgiveness of the townsfolk for all the damage and loss I had caused them when I followed communism. Later, I extended an invitation to those who wanted to accept Christ.

Two young men came up to talk with me. They said they were ready right then to shoot me with a revolver they were carrying. They claimed that, on my orders, many of their friends had died. It was also my fault that the soldiers had killed others of their friends. When they learned I was no longer a guerrilla, they assumed it was safe to kill me. But when they heard me ask forgiveness that night, it caused them to give their lives to Christ, too.

A favourite phrase that university students use these days says that religion is the opiate of the people. The thing is, Marx didn't understand the difference between religion and Christianity. I am totally convinced that the sole reason why I got to Argentina was because God called me there to train and mobilize young people for the mission field. It is a passion that God awakened within my heart.

In December 1993, Jorge married Isabel del Carmen Santamaría, whom he met at the YWAM base in Buenos Aires and who shared his passion for mobilizing young people for the mission field. Jorge and Isabel became the parents of three daughters. In 1998, YWAM commissioned the couple to plant a second school for discipleship and missions in Argentina.

Jorge Rios represents a splendid irony of the Shining Path war. A man who at one time destroyed Christians, on orders from his superiors, now works passionately to spread Christianity on orders from Above. Bruce and Jan Benson, who once nearly died at Jorge's hands, can appreciate better than most the extraordinary change God accomplished in his life. 'For a long time, we couldn't imagine why God allowed that kidnapping to happen,' Jan once told a visiting journalist. 'But then, to see all this was a real faith builder for us. Now we can say, "Thank you Lord, that you gave us a glimpse of some of your purposes for that trip." After all, it was just one day with terrorists.'

*   *   *

Chakiqpampa, September 1999

Of all the meetings Joshua Sauñe and his Runa Simi colleagues organize each year to spread the gospel, none is better attended than the event held in the first week of September to mark the anniversary of his brothers' deaths. Early in his missionary career, it occurred to Joshua that a combination music festival–Bible conference–evangelistic campaign, celebrated in Chakiqpampa, would fittingly commemorate the lives of Rómulo, Ruben, Josué and Marco Antonio, who, like their grandfather Justiniano Quicaña, died at the hands of the Path. The first week of September 1999, some 2,000 people gathered in the village for the commemorative festival, which lasted for several days. The vast majority, of course, were Quechua Christians. Many came from distant communities in other parts of Peru. Some international guests even showed up, despite the risk of attack from the few *senderistas* that still haunted the mountains of rural Huamanga. All were made to feel welcome. All except for one.

'Look, Joshua, *El Anka* is coming,' Carlos Trisollini said, edging closer to his friend. The two were sitting together within a circle of civilian militia. Because of the lingering risk of terrorist attack, militiamen came to the September festival armed. As he spoke to Joshua, Carlos's hand moved to clutch his gun.

Joshua looked up and saw the man, yet far away but plainly walking in the direction of Chakiqpampa. The civilian militia straightened up, watching intently the approach of El Anka, hands clutching their guns.

'He is coming straight toward you, Joshua,' somebody said.

'Let him come.' Joshua hoped his even tone would ease the tension. It did not.

Joshua had learned about El Anka from Carlos, who made it his business to keep tabs on the few *senderistas* still lingering in the mountains of rural Huamanga. Carlos said El Anka had held high rank in the Path, that he had killed many, many Christians and that they feared him still. 'El Anka is very cunning,' Carlos added. 'He knows how to disguise himself to avoid detection while he stalks his prey.'

El Anka had attended the Chakiqpampa festival the year before, disguised by a long beard. Joshua did not know at the time who the man was, but in his spirit he sensed malice emanating from the stranger who walked into the Bible conference he was teaching. Nevertheless, Joshua made the stranger feel welcome.

'Sit down please, Brother,' he said. 'Have you received the teaching materials? Here, these are for you.'

Without a word, the stranger took the materials from Joshua and sat. And though he listened attentively to the Bible teaching, the odd sensation of enmity did not leave Joshua until the man departed. Carlos's habit of keeping tabs on the few *senderistas* in rural Huamanga eventually revealed what lay behind Joshua's puzzling encounter with the bearded stranger.

'El Anka has been trying to kill you for a long time,' Carlos told his friend one day. 'That's why he came to your Bible conference to hear what you had to say.'

'But nobody is going to kill you,' Carlos added. 'They're going to have to kill me first, before they get you.' He repeatedly said this to assure Joshua of his vigilance.

Joshua repeatedly thanked his friend for his vigilance and added, 'Carlos, remember, I'm not doing my business here in this world. I'm doing the business of the Lord. If he wants, he will take me home.'

Joshua and Carlos both wondered what the Lord might want to do this September day as they sat watching El Anka approach Chakiqpampa. After some time, Joshua spoke to the civilian militia surrounding him. 'It's all right, we can see that he's not armed. I don't think he's going to do anything with everybody watching. Let him come.'

El Anka came directly up to the knot of armed men. 'Hello, brother Joshua, can I sit beside you?' he said.

Joshua looked directly into the man's eyes, but could not detect the malice that had attended their first encounter. 'Please, sit down,' he said evenly. El Anka sat down.

'Brother Joshua, I have a confession to make,' he said.

'What is it?'

'Well, I don't know if you know, but I've been trying to kill you for the longest time.'

Carlos's hand did not move from his gun. The militiamen straightened again, intently watching the man's every move.

'I have sent people to get you,' El Anka continued, 'but I always failed.'

Joshua glanced at Carlos, who nodded slightly. Had he not, just weeks before at an evangelistic campaign, cautioned Joshua that three strangers in the crowd were *senderistas* bent on assassinating him? They failed to carry out their plan, of course, thanks to Carlos's vigilance and, evidently, because the Lord did not yet want to take Joshua home.

El Anka spoke again. 'A month ago, I got sick. So sick that they took me to the doctor in Ayacucho. But he couldn't do anything. I was dying. But I remembered last year, when I came to see you – probably you didn't know, but I came to see you when you were teaching.'

Joshua smiled slightly, but said nothing.

'You talked about how Jesus can heal, that he has the power to do that. So, at the time I'm thinking I am going to die, I told them to call a pastor. The pastor came with other brothers. I asked them to pray for me. They prayed and I got healed. So I accepted Jesus Christ, too. I'm a changed man now. I came here to ask you to forgive me.'

Joshua chose his words carefully. 'I knew what you were trying to do,' he said, 'but I trusted the Lord. To me, today is a special day because I see the Lord has changed your heart. So if you are a believer like me, let us work together. I know your desire has been to change our country. That's my desire, too. Let's both teach the gospel of our Lord, so that our country will change.'

'But, do you forgive me?' El Anka asked again.

'The Lord has forgiven you,' Joshua said, 'and he forgave me, too. Who am I not to forgive? Of course, I forgive you. You are my brother.'

With that, the two men shook hands. The tension hanging over the knot of armed men eased. El Anka smiled and stood to go. Then he said, 'Ah, one more thing, brother Joshua. Can my children come to your school?'

'Do you mean, the Rómulo Sauñe Primary School?'

'Yes, I think they need to learn about Christ, too.'

Joshua smiled. 'Of course.'